THE GR-EIGHTEST!

MANCHESTER UNITED HAVE PICKED UP EIGHT CHAMPIONSHIP WINS IN THE 11 YEARS OF THE PREMIERSHIP. HERE'S HOW THEY ACHIEVED THEIR AMAZING SUCCESS.

1 1992-93
22 TEAMS

MARK HUGHES, (right) now Wales manager, fired 15 goals and was United's top league scorer as The Red Devils made the very first Premiership title theirs.

Not a lot of goals, but add nine each from Eric Cantona, Ryan Giggs and Brian McClair and you can see just how dangerous they were all over the field.

Amazingly, four players were ever-present through all 42 league games: McClair, Gary Pallister, Peter Schmeichel and Steve Bruce.

Man United	**84 pts**
Aston Villa	74 pts
Norwich City	72 pts

2 1993-94
22 TEAMS

KING CANTONA (above left) grabbed 18 goals and turned on the French charm has he fired United to a record points total.

But let's not forget that Giggsy also managed to up his scoring rate to 13 and Sparky added another dozen. Only Republic of Ireland full-back Denis Irwin managed to play in every game for the team.

Man United	92
Blackburn	84
Newcastle	77

3 1995-96
20 TEAMS

ERIC THE GREAT was once again Man United's top man in front of goal with 14 – three more than Andy Cole who had joined the side from their nearest challengers this season, Newcastle. Ryan Giggs also hit 11 but not one United player managed to play in every single game.

Man United	84
Newcastle	78
Liverpool	71

4 1996-97
20 TEAMS

IT WAS THE TURN of Ole Gunnar Solskjaer to hit the goalscoring heights with 18, a figure that made him the league's joint third scorer with Robbie Fowler. But once again, Eric (above) the goalden boy weighed in with 11 goals and a certain Mr Beckham got lucky seven for Sir Alex's men.

Man United	75
Newcastle	68
Arsenal	68
(goal difference)	

To Ben
Love
Auntie Janice

CARLING CHAMPIONS 1998-99

CARLING CHAMPIONS 1998-99

5 1998-99
20 TEAMS

THIS WAS THE SEASON the Dwight Yorke and Andy Cole partnership notched up 18 and 17 goals respectively. Add another dozen from Solskjaer and it also meant that United were on their way to being the Premiership's top scorers that season with 53.

Man United	79
Arsenal	78
Chelsea	75

CARLING CHAMPIONS
AGAIN & AGAIN & AGAIN & AGAIN & AGAIN

CARLING CHAMPIONS

6 1999-2000
20 TEAMS

JUST ONE POINT SHORT of their own Premiership points record, despite there now being 20 teams in the division – and 18 points away from their nearest challengers!
Yorkey with 20 and Cole (right) with 19, plus Solskjaer with his usual dozen saw United just three goals short of the 100 over the season.

Man United	91
Arsenal	73
Leeds	69

7 2000-01
20 TEAMS

THE NEW MILLENNIUM saw nothing new at the top of the Premiership with United still edging out their big rivals Arsenal, although the points gap had narrowed since the previous season. Teddy Sheringham (below) knocked in a club's season best 15 goals but another ten went in via... yes, you guessed it, Mr Reliable Ole Gunnar Solskjaer.

Man United	80
Arsenal	70
Liverpool	69

8 2002-03
20 TEAMS

THE PUNDITS RECKONED they couldn't do it, no way could they come back from an indifferent start. Come on! We are talking Man United here, you really should know better!

A few quick boots flung across the dressing room, a few kicks up the backside and everything was back to normal. Oh, and they were helped in no mean fashion by the Golden Boot winner Ruud van Nistelrooy - £19m well spent.

Man United	83
Arsenal	78
Newcastle	69

WHEN THEY FAILED

- 1994-95 United were pushed into second place by just one point, overtaken by the Kenny Dalglish managed Blackburn Rovers.
- 1997-98 Arsenal also pipped Man United by a single point as they did a League and FA Cup double.
- 2001-02 Another Arsenal double and a rare season without a single trophy for Old Trafford.

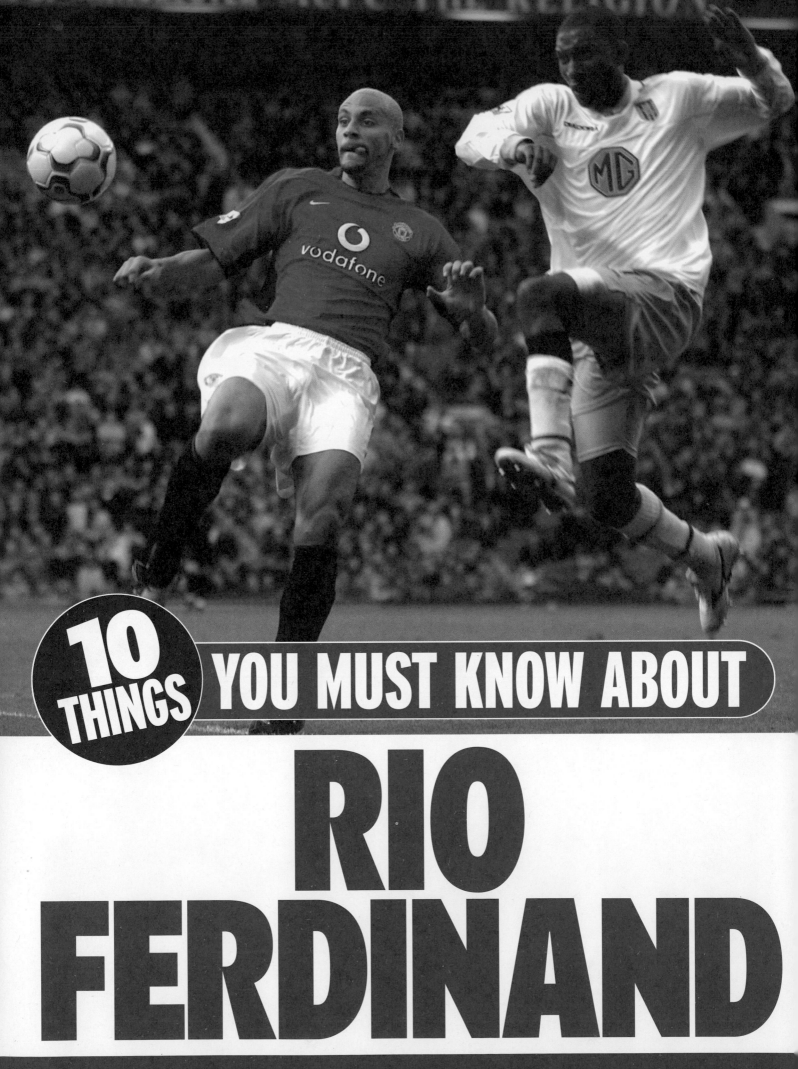

10 THINGS
YOU MUST KNOW ABOUT
RIO FERDINAND

JUST WHO IS THE MAN UNITED AND ENGLAND DEFENDER?

1 Rio Gavin Ferdinand was born on November 7, 1978 in Peckham, South East London (Del Boy country).

2 Football was already in the Ferdinand family as second cousin Les has played for QPR, Newcastle, Spurs and West Ham. Rio's younger brother Anton is with The Hammers.

3 Rio was probably not too pleased when his dad revealed that he did ballet as a youngster! Apparently Rio was a ballet dancer as a kid and cried when he had to give it up at the age of nine! Today his other interests include tennis, table tennis and basketball. His favourite player is Michael Jordan.

American basketball star Michael Jordan is a big hero of Rio's.

4 Unsurprisingly, given his skill on the ball, Rio started out as a centre-forward for local side Bloomfields. His 30-goals-a-season soon saw him switch to junior team, Eltham Town.

5 He joined West Ham as a 14-year-old and despite interest from Middlesbrough, Norwich City, Millwall, Charlton Athletic and Chelsea Rio signed on a £30 per week YTS contract. Unfortunately, Rio's childhood favourite team Liverpool didn't show a desire to take him to Anfield.

6 While cleaning Hammers' legendary striker Tony Cottee's boots Rio helped the West Ham youth team win the South East Counties League in 1996 with a record number of points. He signed a professional contract at just 17. Rio was then sent out to Bournemouth on loan in November 1996 and in January 1997. To this day he maintains that it was the biggest learning experience of his sporting life.

7 Later in 1997 he became a West Ham regular, breaking into Peter Taylor's England Under-21 squad and then made his full debut against Cameroon. A year later he made Glenn Hoddle's Word Cup squad but did not get a game. Kevin Keegan left him out of Euro 2000.

8 West Ham accepted a British record-breaking £18m bid from Leeds in 2000 to make him the most expensive defender in the world. After a superb World Cup that record was again broken when he signed for Manchester United. His £30m fee beat that set by Juan Sebastian Veron (£28m) in the UK and the World's most expensive defender, Lilian Thuram (£22m). He is now said to earn approximately £6.8m a year!

9 Although a single man, Rio has already given some thought to the name of his first child: "I am thinking of calling it 'Romario'. Partly because it is a different name, because he was a legend on the football field (Brazilian striker) and also because it includes my name 'Rio' at the end. That is the plan at the moment. I don't want to have a normal, boring name for my kids."

10 10. According to his personal website Rio lists BBC's John Motson and Sky TV's Martin Tyler as his favourite commentators. His preferred stadium is... you've guessed... Old Trafford!

Brazil ace Romario could help Rio name his first child.

COMPLIMENTS OF THE
SEASON

WINNING ISN'T EVERYTHING BUT IT CERTAINLY HELPS! THESE TEAMS AND PLAYERS FINISHED 2002-2003 ON TOP OF THE WORLD.

PORTSMOUTH
DIVISION ONE CHAMPIONS

Harry Redknapp's wheeling and dealing during the summer really paid off. Paul Merson was inspirational after his surprise move from Aston Villa. Pompey were in a different class as they bounced back to the top flight for the first time in 16 years. They were joined in the automatic promotion places by Micky Adams' Leicester City, who battled on despite crippling financial problems to bounce straight back to the Premiership after the previous season's relegation. Wolves finally got back their place in the top league after 19 years away thanks to a 3-0 victory over Sheffield United in the play-off final at Cardiff's Millennium Stadium.

WIGAN ATHLETIC
DIVISION TWO CHAMPIONS

Paul Jewell was named the division's Manager of Season as his Wigan Athletic side took the crown by 14 clear points. The Latics' cause was certainly helped by striker Nathan "Duke" Ellington who fired in 22 of the goals that sealed promotion. Meanwhile, Crewe Alexandra took the automatic promotion spot to bounce back to Division One, led by the longest-serving manager in England, Dario Gradi. Cardiff City were promoted via the play off final with a 1-0 extra-time victory over QPR.

YEOVIL TOWN
CONFERENCE CHAMPIONS

No more non-league giant-killing acts for Yeovil who won the Conference with a record 95 points to get into the Football League for the first time in their history. Doncaster, who have been there before, got the next promotion spot with a 3-2 extra-time play off final win over unlucky Dagenham and Redbridge, who missed out the previous season only on goal difference.

RUSHDEN & DIAMONDS
DIVISION THREE CHAMPIONS

The final day clash between Hartlepool and Rushden decided the title and saw Diamonds gain the trophy and title in only their second season in the top flight. Hartlepool, unlucky to miss out on promotion over the past few years, got the runner-up spot, despite losing boss Chris Turner mid-season. Former Blackburn striker Mike Newell continued his good work. Wrexham, the division's top scorers, went straight back up at the first attempt with Bournemouth sealing the final promotion place with a 5-2 play off win over Lincoln.

BURSCOUGH
FA TROPHY WINNERS

The under-dogs from Merseyside beat Tamworth 2-1 in the final in front of a 14,265 crowd at Villa Park, led by former Villa star Shaun Teale.

BRISTOL CITY
LDV VANS TROPHY

Bristol missed out on promotion to Division One but took some comfort in the LDV Vans win over Carlisle.

RANGERS
SCOTTISH PREMIER CHAMPIONS, SCOTTISH AND LEAGUE CUPS

Rangers completed a week of misery for Celtic, taking the Premiership crown on the final day by virtue of goals scored. Just days earlier The Bhoys had missed out in Europe. Rangers also collected the Scottish Cup with a 1-0 win over Dundee and the League Cup defeating Celtic 2-1 in the final.

BRIGG TOWN
FA VASE WINNERS

Some 6,634 people saw Brigg Town beat AFC Sudbury 2-1.

LIVERPOOL
WORTHINGTON CUP

A 2-0 win over Manchester United gave the Anfield lads their only silverware of what was a difficult season and at least ensured European football.

ARSENAL
FA CUP

Gunners' boss Arsene Wenger said that winning the FA Cup would mean little after missing out of the league title. Who was he trying to kid? The 1-0 win over Southampton meant more silverware at Highbury.

FC PORTO
UEFA CUP

Martin O'Neill became the first Celtic manager for 33 years to take The Bhoys to a European final. They can justifiably claim that some of the refereeing decision were not great, but they were still beaten by Porto.

JERMAINE JENAS
PFA YOUNG PLAYER OF THE YEAR

A teenager at the turn of the year, his 20th birthday on the same day as his club boss turned 70, young Jermaine thoroughly deserved his title. Capped it all with a call up to the full England squad.

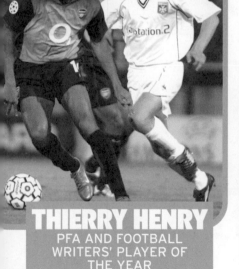

THIERRY HENRY
PFA AND FOOTBALL WRITERS' PLAYER OF THE YEAR

Described as the best player on the planet, the flying Frenchman plays down his contribution to the team. He not only scores a heap of goals, but he also creates them for his team-mates. Truly a season of va, va voom.

AC MILAN
UEFA CHAMPIONS LEAGUE

The all-Italian final with Juventus saw AC's Paolo Maldini follow in the footsteps of his father as he lifted the trophy in England 40 years after Dad Cesare.

BATTLE OF THE

CHRIS KIRKLAND V DAVID SEAMAN

ENGLAND OFTEN STRUGGLE for a goalkeeper or appear to have loads available at the same time. Just when it looked like there would be problems replacing Seaman as his career neared its end, up popped Liverpool's Chris Kirkland as the country's big hope. But his route to the Anfield first-team was blocked by Jerzy Dudek before the Polish keeper lost form. Chris grabbed the No.1 shirt but then suffered a long-term injury that held up his progress. We've all seen enough to know that Chris, who cost £8m, will be a more than serious contender to take over from Man City recruit Seaman, who has been reliable with a few faults.

VERDICT: KIRKLAND 9 SEAMAN 9

WAYNE BRIDGE V CHRIS POWELL

CHARLTON'S CHRIS POWELL didn't make his full England debut until he was in his 30s, but he proved so useful that it makes you wonder what he could have done in his younger days, given a chance. Just like Chris, Wayne was with an unfashionable team when he made his international breakthrough, but the Southampton defender showed no nerves and bombed forwards at every opportunity. He can obviously improve his game further, but the talent is there and all he needs is the experience. Until last season he also had the massive bonus of being a player who manages to avoid injuries.

VERDICT: BRIDGE 8 POWELL 7

STEVE FINNAN V JEFF KENNA

JEFF KENNA HAS been around so long, and in the top flight for most of his career, that you tend to forget just how useful a player he can be. He proved his worth as Blackburn won the Premiership title and played a big part in making sure that Birmingham's arrival in the Premiership was a successful one. Strong and determined, a grafter. Steve Finnan's move to Liverpool from Fulham could be just the springboard he needs for more experience. Mind you, after a successful 2002 World Cup Finals for the Republic of Ireland, the raiding defender, who can also play midfield, is already a star.

VERDICT: FINNAN 9 KENNA 7

AGES

HERE'S WHAT COULD HAPPEN IF A TEAM OF RISING YOUNG STARS TAKES ON A SIDE OF OLDIES BUT GOODIES FROM BRITISH FOOTBALL. WE KNOW YOU CAN'T REALLY COMPARE, BUT IT IS A FUNNY OLD GAME. OLD AND NEW MANAGERS TOO!

RIO FERDINAND V MARTIN KEOWN

MANY OF ENGLAND'S promising young professionals now look up to Rio as the man they respect. The country's most expensive transfer, following moves from West Ham to Leeds (£18m) and then onto Man United (£29m) opened people's eyes. Still needs to improve his concentration, but his best years are probably still to come. Loves to play the ball out of defence rather than just hoof up the pitch. Martin Keown might not win any prizes as a pin-up and he may make a few tackles that could be questioned, but there's no denying the major part he has played at Arsenal during two spells with the club.

VERDICT: FERDINAND 9 KEOWN 9

LEDLEY KING V GARETH SOUTHGATE

GARETH SOUTHGATE IS simply Mr Reliable. Any player who misses a vital penalty for his country then allows himself to be laughed at in a pizza advert about the miss has to be an okay guy.
But more importantly, Gareth, who converted from a midfielder during his time at Aston Villa, is a defender who can play, tidy up mistakes, win balls in the air and even get up to the opposition penalty box. Ledley is a young player with a lot of promise and could, at times, be likened to the man whose place he took in the Spurs side, Sol Campbell. Still needs to improve, but has time on his side.

VERDICT: KING 7 SOUTHGATE 8

JERMAINE JENAS V GARY SPEED

GARY SPEED JUST GOT BETTER WITH AGE! But Jermaine Jenas (that pronounced Gee-nas now!) could leave the old master standing. JJ has total respect for his Newcastle team-mate, but within the next few years he is expected to be one of the biggest stars in world football. He'll have learnt from one of the best on the pitch and one of the best off it, his manager Bobby Robson. Speedo does his job and helps out with a few wonder goals, including some powerful headers. JJ is going to have to improve his scoring ratio and learn a bit more about using his head before he can be as good as the Welshman.

VERDICT: JENAS 9 SPEED 8

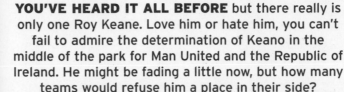

YOU'VE HEARD IT ALL BEFORE but there really is only one Roy Keane. Love him or hate him, you can't fail to admire the determination of Keano in the middle of the park for Man United and the Republic of Ireland. He might be fading a little now, but how many teams would refuse him a place in their side? Scotty shows the same determination as Keano, even though he may not yet have the same strength and experience. Charlton could be his launching pad for bigger and better things, including a lengthy England career. Appears everywhere across the middle of the park and can pop in the occasional wonder goal.

VERDICT: PARKER 8 KEANE 9

STEVEN GERRARD  MARK KINSELLA

LIVERPOOL BOSS GERARD HOULLIER reckons that if he had five or six more players like Stevie Gerrard he would be happy. He would be more than happy - his side would be world-beaters!
The England midfielder snaps like a crocodile in midfield and can slide through amazing passes or deliver long balls with ease. He's also got a blistering shot that can leave goalkeepers standing. His only downfall could be his sometimes short temper.
Mark Kinsella was a driving force at Charlton before he moved to Villa and always Mr Dependable when he pulled on the green shirt of the Republic of Ireland.

VERDICT: GERRARD 9 KINSELLA 7

JOE COLE  TEDDY SHERINGHAM

STEADY TEDDY is a one-off, a player with vision who could make a great move into management when he finally hangs up his boots. Millwall and Forest appreciated his skills, as did Spurs before he went to Manchester United to really prove his worth. A second spell at Tottenham might not have been so great, but remember he was still turning it on for England in his mid-30s. Creative, a great header, a superb link man and a goalscorer. What can you ask? Joe Cole has bags of skills and a neat collection of tricks. He can be outstanding and experience might just give him the consistency he needs for England.

VERDICT: COLE 8 SHERINGHAM 9

SUBS YOUNG STARS
MATT OAKES, JAMES MILNER, SHOLA AMEOBI, ASHLEY COLE, KEVIN NOLAN

SUBS OLDIES BUT GOODIES
DAVE BEASANT, JIMMY FLOYD HASSELBAINK, MARCEL DESAILLY, PAUL MERSON, GUS POYET

TOTAL
Oldies but goodies 101.5
The young ones 100

FRANNY JEFFERS V GIANFRANCO ZOLA

NO-ONE IS PERFECT but we simply had to give Zola top marks because of his skill, commitment, loyalty to Chelsea and the entertainment he always gives. A great ball player with excellent vision, great speed despite being nearer 40 than 30, and a true pro who still amazes his colleagues with his attitude to training and life in general. A creator as well as scorer. Franny hasn't had the best of luck since his £11m move from Everton to Arsenal and his future always appears to have a question mark over it, but there's no denying that when he gets the ball anywhere near the box he is a major danger. Just needs a chance to play.

VERDICT: JEFFERS 8 ZOLA 10

WAYNE ROONEY V ALAN SHEARER

WRITTEN OFF more times than a stock car banger, Alan Shearer has always defied his critics to bounce back from career-threatening injuries and poor form. We are not going to put him out to graze just yet. At the age of 33 he can still be a major force, can still bang in those important goals, and be a nuisance. Watch how many times he holds the ball up until support arrives, and how often he defends. We've given Wayne the wonder boy nine out of ten based on his first season in the Premiership with Everton but reckon he could hit ten. Bags of natural skill, powerful and no worries, even at the age of 17!

VERDICT: WAYNE ROONEY 9 SHEARER 9.5

DAVID PLATT V SIR BOBBY ROBSON

KNOWING SIR BOBBY he would probably have preferred it if we let him manage our team of youngsters - just look at the average age of the side he has built at Newcastle! But if he wants to join in with the spirit of our challenge he has to take on the Oldies. Even at the age of 70 we reckon he can knock any half-decent side into shape, so given the experienced old hands we've given him here, plus a couple of United players, we reckon there are no problems. England Under-21 boss Platty, who has had experience playing abroad and also managing Nottingham Forest, has made no secret of the fact that he wants to take over the senior side from Sven Goran Eriksson, so we are giving him the chance to manage a potentially great side and see just how he can do. Okay, we admit that at least in the battle of the bosses Platty is going to have his work cut out, but he has got youth on his side. We still think the older hand might give him a major run for his money after working in Spain, Holland and Portugal.

VERDICT: PLATT 7 SIR BOBBY 9

SHOOT'S A TO Z OF
WORLD STARS

(A) PABLO AIMAR

ARGENTINA PLAYMAKER who signed for Spanish side Valencia in January 2001 for £13m. He is the link between midfield and attack with clever movement and quick feet. Not the first Argentine to be labelled "the new Maradona" and probably won't be the last either!

(B) RAUL GONZALEZ BLANCO

The golden boy of Spanish football. Raul burst on to the scene at the age of 17 and has never looked back – becoming the leading scorer in the Champions League. His partnership with Ronaldo for Real is simply formidable.

(C) SANTIAGO CANIZARES

THE GOALKEEPER is a real rock for the Spanish national side and also for his club Valencia. Unfortunately, he missed the 2002 World Cup after dropping a bottle of aftershave on his foot, severing the right tendon! Arguably the best keeper in the world at present.

(D) ALESSANDRO DEL PIERO

DEL PIERO IS NOT dissimilar to Raul in that he is the darling of Italian football and idolised by thousands of fans in Italy and the world. Has been at Juventus now for more than a decade and the Juve fans are attracted to his sublime technique, vision and skill. Has the tendency to hide when the going gets tough.

E SAMUEL ETO'O

THIS 21-YEAR-OLD Cameroon ace has the potential to become a footballing superstar and has already developed an excellent understanding with strike partner, Patrick Mboma. Currently playing at Real Mallorca in Spain.

F LUIS FIGO

PORTUGUESE PLAYMAKER who is a natural winger and with a massive following of fans, some who love him, some who hate him! He sparked controversy and fury after his transfer to deadly rivals Real Madrid from Barcelona for £37m in July 2000.

G NUNO GOMES

RETURNED TO under-achievers Benfica after last summer's embarrassing World Cup Finals. Left debt-ridden Fiorentina after two dismal seasons in Italy. A star at Euro 2000, but hasn't shown any quality since then. May struggle to make the Portugal squad for Euro 2004.

H THIERRY HENRY

THE FRENCHMAN has that rare quality of being a striker who not only scores but provides goals too. He was a teenage star at Monaco and became an integral part of Arsenal's 2002 double-winning side. A World Cup winner in 1998 but four years later France crashed out without scoring a goal.

I ZLATAN IBRAHIMOVIC

SWEDISH STRIKER, Ibrahimovic has been coveted for quite a few seasons by many top European clubs but his controversial reputation and training ground rows have led to his development at Ajax being hindered. One for the future, though.

J JENS JEREMIES

BAYERN MUNICH MIDFIELDER, famous for his tough-tackling and no-nonsense approach to the game. His range of passing has improved over the years. Has been used in defence and midfield for Germany.

K PATRICK KLUIVERT

DUTCH INTERNATIONAL STRIKER. He was the joint top-scorer at Euro 2000 and was disappointed not to have qualified for the World Cup. His goal scoring and disciplinary records at Barcelona aren't really anything to be to proud of but he is always the subject of praise by fellow team-mates. A move to England could also be on the cards.

L JARI LITMANEN

A REAL FOOTBALL ARCHITECT, he is at the centre of most attacking moves and has had a glittering career playing at top clubs such as Ajax, Barca and Liverpool. He is still regarded as an important part of the Finland side.

M PAOLO MALDINI

ONE OF THE GREAT Italian players of all time, and loyal defender with AC Milan, whom he captained to Champions League glory at the end of last season. He is the complete defender and has won 100-plus caps for Italy.

Q QU BO

THE 21-YEAR-OLD China international has a bright future ahead of him. A career in English football seems likely for this all-action striker and as such could become the player to put Chinese football well and truly on the map.

N PAVEL NEDVED

WAS GIVEN THE difficult task of succeeding Zinedine Zidane at Juventus. He possesses great power, accuracy, vision and has an incredible appetite for the game. Captain of the Czech Republic, and hopeful of leading them to Euro 2004 glory next summer.

R RONALDO/RIVALDO RONALDINHO

THE THREE R's of Brazilian football and the three players who really light up the international stage. Without them, Brazil are a good side. With them, they are virtually unbeatable! Unbelievably skillful - take your pick as to who is the best of the bunch.

O JAY JAY OKOCHA

OKOCHA IS EXPLOSIVE, stylish and extremely effective. He has amazing ability and can do tricks with a football that most of us can only dream of. He is the focal point of the Nigerian team but is sometimes criticised for his inconsistency and indulging in too much showmanship.

S ANDREI SCHEVCHENKO

AC MILAN AND Ukraine striker Shevchenko is one of the most under-rated forwards in the game. Scorer of crucial goals for both club and country he netted the winning penalty against Juventus that ensured the Champions League trophy went to AC Milan. A natural predator.

P CARLOS PUYOL

THE SPANIARD has cemented his place at right-back for club and country. Has been at Barcelona since 1999 and was a star of the World Cup Finals in 2002 - despite Spain losing to Korea. His performances have resulted in him being offered an extended contract to stay at Camp Nou until 2006.

T FRANCESCO TOTTI

TOTTI HAS BEEN on a bit of a roller coaster ride recently. Emerged from Euro 2000 as an Italian superstar but has since struggled to match that form for club (Roma) and country. Was controversially sent off against South Korea in the last World Cup as Italy crashed out.

U UMIT DAVALA

TURKISH STAR, Davala, is regarded as one of the best footballers to have ever come out of Turkey. He is quick and versatile and has an uncanny knack of scoring goals in vital matches. One of the stars of Turkey's World Cup Finals.

Y YOO SANG CHUL

THIS PLAYER HAS JUST achieved 100 caps for South Korea and is well-respected in Asia. Another intelligent, versatile player who scored crucial goals in World Cup 2002 to help his side reach the semi-finals.

V RUUD VAN NISTELROOY

THIS DUTCH 'GOAL MACHINE' has been a revelation! After recovering from a career-threatening injury, he finally completed his dream move to Manchester United in July 2001. Before the 2003-2004 campaign had already notched 80 goals in just 100 games.

Z ZINEDINE ZIDANE

WHAT CAN YOU SAY ABOUT ZIZOU! He constantly features in 'All-time Greats' teams and has everything the modern footballer desires. An excellent passer of the ball with an exquisite eye for goal. First pick for France and he still has enough in him to win major trophies at Real Madrid. Forget Ronaldo, Raul and Beckham – Zidane is still the best player in the world today.

W MARC WILMOTS

MARC WILMOTS IS a Belgian international who has been part of three World Cup squads but never enjoyed any real success apart from winning the UEFA Cup with Schalke in 1997. Strong, bullish and very effective as an attacking midfielder. He captains his country.

X XAVI

XAVI IS A PLAYER with a promising future at the Nou Camp. The 23-year-old midfield man has already had a taste of success with Spain Under-20s and looks likely to play a crucial role in helping Barcelona recapture the glory days. Will still be relieved that Becks chose Real over Barca.

WHERE IN THE WORLD?

Look at the six stadiums pictured and say which clubs play their home games there.

A ....

B ....

C ....

D ....

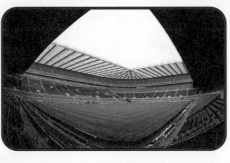

E ....

F ....

SPOT THE BALL

We have removed a ball from the picture below. Place an X where you think it might be.

NAME THE YEAR

Guess the years below from the following clues

YEAR A

1. Steve Bruce (right) became boss of Birmingham City.
2. Michael Owen scored a hat-trick against Germany.
3. Chesterfield had nine points deducted in Division Three but still gained promotion.

YEAR B

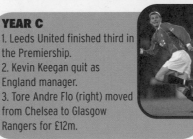

1. David Beckham (right) made his England debut.
2. Borussia Dortmund won the European Cup against Juve.
3. Roberto Di Matteo scored the fastest-ever goal in a FA Cup Final.

YEAR C

1. Leeds United finished third in the Premiership.
2. Kevin Keegan quit as England manager.
3. Tore Andre Flo (right) moved from Chelsea to Glasgow Rangers for £12m.

YEAR D

1. Alan Shearer's Blackburn Rovers (right) were crowned Premiership Champions.
2. Dennis Bergkamp signed for Arsenal.
3. Trevor Francis was sacked as boss of Sheffield Wednesday.

CRAZY?

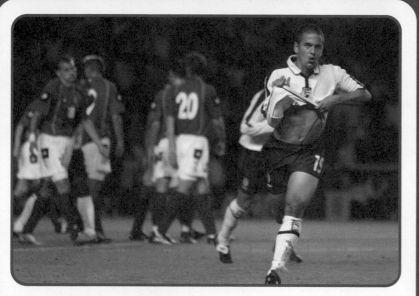

GOAL GRABBER 1

DATE: September 21, 2002
VENUE: Highbury
MATCH: Arsenal v Bolton
RESULT: 2-1
Name the goalscorer from the players listed below:
A. Patrick Vieira
B. Thierry Henry
C. Sylvain Wiltord
D. Nwankwo Kanu

QUICK QUIZ 1

1. Which team beat Celtic in last season's UEFA Cup Final?
2. Name all the clubs that Teddy Sheringham has played for during his 20-year career.
3. What shirt colours do you traditionally associate with Burnley?
4. Mark Hughes used to play for Manchester United, Chelsea and which other Premiership club?
5. Alan Shearer began his professional career at which club?
6. Comedian Bradley Walsh used to be on the books of which London club?
7. Which country will host the European Championships next summer?
8. Name the winners of the first FA Cup Final that was played at the Millennium Stadium, Cardiff.
9. Which two clubs were relegated from the Nationwide League to the Conference last season?
10. England star Joe Cole scored his first international for England against which nation?

SPORTING FANS

Which clubs do the following sports stars support:
A. Colin Montgomerie
B. Frankie Dettori
C. Alec Stewart

NATIONAL TREASURES

Link the following clubs to the countries they play in:

1. Colorado Rapids	Portugal
2. Feyenoord	Germany
3. Lazio	Holland
4. Alaves	Brazil
5. Grasshopper	Greece
6. Benfica	France
7. PAOK	USA
8. Energie Cottbus	Spain
9. Lyon	Switzerland
10. Santos	Italy

WHAT WE DO ON OUR
DAYS OFF

YOU TRAIN IN THE MORNING AND GET THE REST OF THE DAY OFF! HERE'S WHAT SOME FOOTBALL STARS DO IN THEIR SPARE TIME.

STEADY TEDDY. Veteran striker Teddy Sheringham eyes up a long put – but he's not finished playing with the bigger ball just yet!

DON'T JUMP! Striker Bobby Zamora made the best of Brighton by taking in the bracing sea air.

TOP DECK. Chelsea's Dutch hitman Jimmy Floyd Hasselbaink finds time to spin a few discs.

TEEING OFF. England star Michael Owen shows that he's a bit of a dab hand at golf too. Shame about the shorts though!

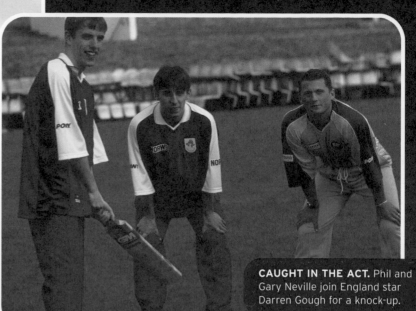

CAUGHT IN THE ACT. Phil and Gary Neville join England star Darren Gough for a knock-up.

GOOD BET. When United boss Sir Alex Ferguson said he was looking for a thoroughbred Ruud van Nistelrooy needn't have worried.

BULLSEYE. Boss Sam Allardyce will be again aiming to keep his Bolton side in the Premiership.

SNOW FUN. Brothers Paul and John Terry lark about in the snow. Paul plays in the Conference for local side Dagenham.

DIGGING DEEP. Birmingham City's Geoff Horsfield just loves a spot of garden improvement.

HOT STUFF. You'd think Man United multi-millionaire Rio Ferdinand could afford to pay someone to cook his breakfast.

YOUNG LIONS

WHO ARE THE NEXT GENERATION OF ENGLAND STARS READY TO MAKE THE BREAKTHROUGH TO THE BIG-TIME?

MICHAEL DAWSON
● NOTTS FOREST ● DEFENDER ● Nov 18, 1983

MICHAEL DAWSON is one of three brothers who all began their careers with Forest. The two elder Dawsons have already departed from the City Ground to lower divisions, but Michael is being tipped for a big money move to the Premiership.

The Yorkshire-born central defender's big hero is Rio Ferdinand and there are already signs in his game that compare favourably to the Manchester United and England defender.

Strong in the air, Michael also likes to play the ball out of defence and he has a knack of being in the right place at the right time at set-pieces which should bring him a few goals.

Has benefited enormously from playing alongside veteran former England defender Des Walker and his progress last season, his first in the league, was outstanding.

CARLTON COLE
● CHELSEA ● STRIKER ●
November 12, 1983

SEASON 2002-2003 was Carlton's headline-hitting season when he scored some vital goals for The Blues, often after coming off the bench.

The youngster showed no respect for Premiership reputations and it looked like he had played in the big time for years.

But Bridge boss Claudio Ranieri eased him gently into the picture and loaned him out for a short spell to Wolves so that he gained more experience.

So much is expected of the London-born striker that he was given a new five-year deal last summer with two years still to run on his old one.

GLEN JOHNSON

● **WEST HAM** ● **DEFENDER**
● **August 23, 1984**

IT WASN'T a happy 2002-2003 season for relegated West Ham but one of the brighter spots was the breakthrough of defender Glen Johnson.

With the club from schoolboy days, he finally got a first-team squad number last season, after he had skippered England Under-19s at the 2002 European Cup.

A tough tackler who works his way out of defence with the ball he also had a short spell on loan with Millwall towards the end of 2002.

He finished the season with 16 appearances, plus eight for Millwall in Division One.

KIERON RICHARDSON

● **MANCHESTER UNITED** ●
MIDFIELDER ● **October 21, 1984**

JUST WHEN it looked like The Red Devils were running out of new youngsters, Kieron Richardson announced his arrival.

The United Youth team product is already a member of the England Under-19 squad and signed a new long-term deal at Old Trafford last season.

Kieron went on to make a total of 12 appearances, three as a substitute, and scored one goal. Can play in central or wide midfield and is highly rated by the United coaching staff. The Greenwich, South East London-born youngster began his career with West Ham but was signed by United boss Sir Alex Ferguson in August 2002.

LIAM RIDGEWELL

● **ASTON VILLA** ●
DEFENDER ● **July 21, 1984**

HE TRAINS WITH the legendary Ireland defender Steve Staunton and has even been likened to the the Republic's most-capped player.

Some praise, but Liam is aware of just how much that means and admits that if he achieves just half of what Staunton has he will have done very well.

Started his playing life as a striker, and moved back from midfield to defence following an injury. Reckons that he has now found his true position and that he won't be moving back even further and into goal!

Another big admirer of Rio Ferdinand who already has an FA Youth Cup victory to his name.

MICHAEL CHOPRA

● **NEWCASTLE UNITED** ● **STRIKER**
● **December 23, 1983**

UNITED MANAGER Bobby Robson has already labelled Michael as "the new Alan Shearer" so he's got an awful lot to live up to!

Chops has scored bags full of goals at whatever level he has played at since joining The Magpies as a schoolboy. Last season he was finally given a squad number and made a couple of cameo appearances as his manager eased him into the side.

Went on a month's loan to Watford towards the end of the 2002-2003 season to gain valuable league experience and banged in four goals during a match at Burnley and played in the FA Cup semi-final.

Fast, strong and with a natural eye for goal, Geordie fans have been awaiting his arrival in the first-team with a sense of great anticipation.

OUR BEST TOP TENS

THE WINNERS OF **SHOOT MONTHLY**'S EXCLUSIVE TOP TEN CHARTS. SEE IF YOU AGREE WITH OUR SELECTIONS.

MANAGER
BRIAN CLOUGH
HARTLEPOOL (1965-67), DERBY (1967-1973), BRIGHTON (1973-74), LEEDS (1974), NOTTINGHAM FOREST (1975-93)

OKAY HE HASN'T won most trophies and he hasn't worked for the biggest clubs in the land, but for sheer entertainment value, Cloughie is our No.1 boss.

Old Big 'Ead was (and is) an interviewer's nightmare – "don't interrupt me when I'm talking" – and woe betide any player who didn't toe the line.

Back in 1972, he and assistant Peter Taylor (pictured right) helped an unfashionable Derby side to the old Division One title.

A 44-day spell at Leeds showed the unpredictable side of Cloughie before he moved on to his spiritual home at Forest.

Over 18 years he took another small club to dizzy heights – a league championship and TWO European Cup triumphs.

Even relegation in his final season could not dim the legend of Brian Clough.

Honours: Nottingham Forest League Cup (1978, 1979, 1989, 1990), championship (1977-78) European Cup (1979, 1980); DERBY: Championship (1971-72)

FOREIGN IMPORT
PATRICK VIEIRA, ARSENAL

ANOTHER GEM unearthed by Arsene Wenger, Patrick Vieira cost Arsenal just £3m from AC Milan in 1996.

And what a piece of business that proved to be! Now established as the premier midfielder of his type in the world, the Euro 2000 and World Cup-winner played a key role in both of Arsenal's recent Double triumphs.

He confounded his critics by putting his disciplinary problems to one side for the good of Arsenal and now proudly wears the captain's armband.

Vieira's Highbury team-mate Dennis Bergkamp reckons: "Patrick has the ability to attack and defend, and that gives us so much more power. He is just an awesome footballer."

PREMIERSHIP VETERAN
GARY SPEED
LEEDS, EVERTON, NEWCASTLE
376 APPEARANCES (64 GOALS)

ONE OF THE UNSUNG performers in the Premiership, Gary Speed is the rock on which much of Newcastle's recent success has been built.

Forming an impenetrable wall in front of the defence but still able to bomb forward to score his fair share of goals, the Welsh captain is one of the first names on Sir Bobby Robson's team sheet.

He began his career at Leeds as a trainee, signing pro in 1988 and going on to spend a further eight years at Elland Road.

After winning the old Division One title in 1991-92 Gary was a virtual ever-present in Leeds' first three Premiership campaigns before being sold to Everton.

However, £3.5m and two seasons later, The Toffees were still underperforming and Newcastle's Kenny Dalglish paid £5.5m to secure his services.

After a slow start and the departure of both Dalglish and Ruud Gullit, Gary is now the fulcrum of Newcastle's on-going Premiership assault and a vital part of the Wales set-up.

FA CUP SHOCKS
HEREFORD V NEWCASTLE 1972
THIRD ROUND REPLAY 2-1

THE MAGIC OF THE FA CUP! Today, the thought of a non-league side turning over a Premiership team seems almost unthinkable but back in the 1970s giant-killing acts were a much more regular occurrence.

But even so... Early on all looked rosy for Joe Harvey's Newcastle as goal-machine Malcolm Macdonald grabbed an early lead. However, no sooner had the Geordies set their sights on the fourth round, than Hereford striker Ronnie Radford pulled out that now famous and fabulous 30-yarder.

The game went into extra-time and Newcastle could only look on in dismay as Ricky George sealed the tie for the home side. The first non-league side to defeat a league team since 1949.

29 ▶

FOOTBALL RECORD
WORLD IN MOTION - NEW ORDER, 1990, HIGHEST POSITION No.1

BEFORE WORLD IN MOTION, football songs were always about a group of embarrassed, tuneless footballers standing in a studio whining along to some uninspiring backing track.

With lyrics by comedian/ actor/writer Keith Allen and the usual sprinkling of New Order magic, World in Motion upped the ante. A brilliant song in its own right, this No.1 hit also unearthed an unlikely pop star - in Liverpool's John Barnes.

Bravely putting his Anfield Rap horror behind him, Barnsey became the face of World Cup '90 and, allied with his team's brilliant showing on the pitch, helped that particular football summer seem one of the best-ever.

NUMBER SEVEN
GEORGE BEST (1963-84)
MAN UNITED, DUNSTABLE TOWN, STOCKPORT COUNTY, LA AZTECS, CORK CELTIC, FULHAM, FORT LAUDERDALE, MOTHERWELL, HIBERNIAN, SAN JOSE EATHQUAKES, BOURNEMOUTH AFC

FOR THE COMPLETE PACKAGE - ability, flair, wit and off-field dramas it had to be Besty.

After making his Man United debut in 1963 at the age of 17, he went on to 361 league appearances and score 137 goals. He helped United to the title in 1964-65 and 1966-67 and also the 1968 European Cup.

George's brand of football - teasing the opposition with pace, guile and breath-taking ball skills - soon helped him to the 1968 Footballer of the Year and European Footballer of the Year awards.

Away from the game he was the first bona fide football superstar, attracting headlines for his celebrity lifestyle, much like Becks 25 years later. A string of disciplinary upsets, saw him leave United and initially retire at the age of 27. Later spells at clubs here and abroad came to nothing but today he remains a true legend.

BAD BOY
DENNIS WISE
WIMBLEDON, CHELSEA, LEICESTER, MILLWALL

DENNIS WISE is certainly something of a handful. A regular sufferer of the red mist, Dennis' career is littered with examples of how not to win friends and influence people.

From losing the Chelsea captaincy due to disciplinary problems, to receiving a three month sentence for assaulting a taxi driver (he was later acquitted) in 1995, it's been pretty much the same story.

And let's not forget the accusations of biting an opponent in Chelsea's 1999 Cup Winners Cup semi-final against Real Mallorca!

Sent home from Leicester's Finland pre-season training camp after breaking team-mate Callum Davidson's jaw in a brawl, he left Filbert Street under a cloud. Now keeping his nose clean at Millwall.

TOO GOOD TO GO DOWN?
WEST HAM 2002-2003

WE JUST HAD TO PLUMP for this mini-soap opera. Temper tantrums (step forward Paolo Di Canio), shock but ultimately disappointing transfers (Gary Breen and Lee Bowyer) and serious illness (boss Glenn Roeder) all within a club who believed the season only really ran from January to May.

A campaign of high drama that not even the best efforts of Les Ferdinand and Irons' stand-in manager Trevor Brooking could rescue. No home wins until January 29 and a defence with more holes than a golf course, meant "superstars" Joe Cole, Michael Carrick, Trevor Sinclair, David James, Christian Dailly and Tomas Repka, would rally too little too late.

ENGLAND NIGHTMARES
ENGLAND V EVERYBODY PENALTIES
1990-2002

SOUTHGATE, BATTY, INCE, WADDLE, PEARCE - all fine players in their own right who will forever be associated with the nightmare of missed penalties.

It all started back in that memorable World Cup of 1990 in which England reached the last four of the tournament for the first time since 1966. In the semi-final against West Germany (who else) we had drama, goal-mouth action and Gazza's tears but the game finished 1-1. Chris Waddle and Stuart Pearce became the fall-guys in a tense penalty shoot-out and England missed out on the final.

Six years later, again against Germany, in the European Champs. A 1-1 draw and a fruitless Golden Goal period saw Gareth Southgate (right) step up in the semi-final shoot-out at Wembley and the centre-half hit the ball straight at the keeper.

In World Cup 1998 against Argentina there was a 2-2 draw, including one of the best England World Cup goals ever by Michael Owen, but marred by Beckham's sending off. The penalty shoot-out saw both Ince and finally Batty fail to score.

PREMIERSHIP HOTSHOT
ALAN SHEARER,
BLACKBURN ROVERS, NEWCASTLE
390 APPEARANCES (221 GOALS)

LOVE HIM OR LOATHE HIM you just can't argue with Big Al's track record. Despite suffering potentially career-threatening injuries he had managed to score a stunning 221 goals in only 390 appearances – and let's not forget he almost single-handedly helped Premiership new boys Blackburn win the title.

Yes he takes all of the penalties and most of the free-kicks and he may not be quite as sprightly as he once was, but ask yourself: who would you want lurking in the box if a chance arose?

Now as sharp as ever after retiring from international football (what a clever decision), Alan is enjoying his football more than ever. Bad news for defenders – there's life in the old dog yet!

PICKING YOUR DREAM TEAM

FANTASY FOOTBALL GAMES ARE ALL THE RAGE, BUT HOW DO YOU MANAGE A SUCCESSFUL TEAM?
SHOOT MONTHLY'S PAUL REANEY BEAT OFF THOUSANDS OF OTHER FANS LAST YEAR TO FINISH
RUNNER-UP IN A MAJOR COMPETITION, SO WE ASKED HIM TO REVEAL HIS SECRETS.

HOW MANY TIMES have you heard Sir Alex Ferguson, when explaining a player's dip in form, mutter: "Och, he didnae have a pre-season. Ye cannae blame the lad fo' tha."?

Or it could be Arsene Wenger mumbling "too many games in ze zummer means he deed not 'ave le pre-saison"?

It's the same with Fantasy League – clever managers start their season a long time before the first ball is kicked by keeping an eye on four things over the summer: promoted teams, new faces, player lists and injuries and suspensions.

This pre-season quartet can be the difference between being a Fantasy League Champ or Chump come May. Let's take a look at how you would have started this season.

FOREIGN OBJECTS

YOU'LL ALSO HAVE TO keep an eye on the comings and goings of more unfamiliar names making their way in to the top flight. Last season anyone with Middlesbrough's Geremi got off to a flyer. But be careful, for every Geremi there's a Gilberto Silva (left), Jonathan Blondel and Igor Biscan. Keep an eye on the pre-season performances of some the lesser-known lights jetting in from Spain, Italy, France and beyond.

ON THE UP!

TEAMS LIKE PORTSMOUTH, Leicester and Wolves would be expected to be at their most potent in August and September following promotion to the Premiership and there's often bargains to be had.

It could have been worth considering the likes of Portsmouth's Patrik Berger, Leicester's Paul Dickov or Wolves' Nathan Blake (right), if not for the whole season, for the first month or two at least.

It could even be that one of the newcomers took the Premiership by surprise for a longer spell. Last year Manchester City's Nicolas Anelka (left) easily outscored Dennis Bergkamp, Andy Cole and Eidur Gudjohnsen despite costing considerably less than his more fancied counterparts.

LISTLESS?

LOOK AT HOW THE PLAYER LISTS have been set up. Have the people putting the lists together got it wrong? Last season Harry Kewell, Paul Scholes (right) and Youri Djorkaeff were listed as midfielders despite playing up front, while John Arne Riise, regarded as a full-back, spent much of the season as a virtual left-winger.

TAKING KNOCKS

FINALLY, KEEP AN EYE ON suspensions and injuries. There was no point formulating a masterplan around the free kicks of Boro's Franck Queudrue (below) when he was banned for the first five games of the season.

Craig Bellamy

Thierry Henry

Ian Harte

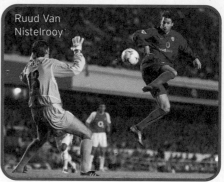

Ruud Van Nistelrooy

PICKING YOUR TEAM

THEY'LL BE EXPENSIVE, but it's very unlikely that you'll get anywhere without Thierry Henry or Ruud Van Nistelrooy.

However, buying both will leave you painfully short of funds for the rest of the team.

It's best to choose one and pair them up with a slightly cheaper option. Kevin Phillips, Frederic Kanoute and Louis Saha have something to prove while young bucks Jermain Defoe, Wayne Rooney and Craig Bellamy won't break the bank and could make big splashes.

At the back, don't pick the best keeper; pick the man who plays behind the best defence. Mark Schwarzer might look like he's waving to his mum at times, but

lining up behind Ugo Ehiogu and Gareth Southgate means he's unlikely to concede vast amounts.

Antti Niemi, Carlo Cudicini and Brad Friedel play behind relatively resilient defences at Southampton, Chelsea and Blackburn and are worth a punt.

Central defenders can be worth their weight in gold. Not only do they get take points for clean sheets, but, from corners and free-kicks, the odd header here and scrambled toe-poke there can add up.

Go for quality. One of Sami Hyypia, Sol Campbell, William Gallas and John O'Shea should be on your shopping list accompanied by a slightly cheaper option; say Stephane Henchoz or Alan Stubbs.

Full-backs are often penalty takers so it's worth considering a David Unsworth or an Ian Harte, while Christian Ziege and Graham Le Saux should provide plenty of crosses and goals. If you're looking to spend big, John Arne Riise will continue to rip his shirt off while sliding on his knees after scoring goals.

It's in the midfield that you should really gamble. Always take a dead cert to make sure your engine room keeps firing, say a Robert Pires, Paul Scholes or Damien Duff.

Elsewhere you have to do your homework; look at attacking midfielders from Tottenham, Charlton, Southampton, Middlesbrough and Fulham.

HE SAID WHAT?

FOOTBALLERS ARE OFTEN ACCUSED OF STATING THE OBVIOUS BUT SOMETIMES THEY SAY A FEW THINGS WHICH ARE A LITTLE MORE INTERESTING. HERE'S WHAT A FEW STAR PLAYERS HAVE ADMITTED TO **SHOOT MONTHLY**.

"I have confidence in my own ability and there are times when I think I am going to score whenever I get the ball in front of goal. But I am also realistic enough to know you can get built up only to be knocked down again. When you are on a good run people automatically presume you have to keep it going, but of course that's not the case. I will always try and remain level-headed and not get too excited or wound-up by any of the hype. You have to take all the attention with a pinch of salt, and I won't allow it to go to my head."
ENGLAND STRIKER **JAMES BEATTIE** REFUSES TO GET BIG-HEADED AFTER 23 GOALS FOR SOUTHAMPTON DURING SEASON 2002-2003.

"How have I played for England? I'd have to say poor! I don't know why that it is because when I'm in an Arsenal shirt I play well but generally when I go out with England I play cr@p! I don't know why. I wouldn't say it was nerves - maybe it's down to playing with different players. Hopefully now that I'm a bit more experienced I'll start to do myself justice and prove the critics wrong. I know how well I can play and I don't think I've come anywhere near that in for England."
ARSENAL AND ENGLAND DEFENDER **ASHLEY COLE** IS BLUNTLY HONEST.

"I am still only 26 - I was the old man of the side when Alan Shearer and Gary Speed were suspended and injured and it was a bit of a scary thought. People say goalkeepers don't peak until they are 29 or 30 so I am hoping that I keep on improving my game. You are always learning and the more experience you gain playing in big games the better."
REPUBLIC OF IRELAND AND NEWCASTLE No.1 SHAY GIVEN REFLECTS ON LIFE IN WHAT IS PROBABLY THE PREMIERSHIP'S YOUNGEST SQUAD.

"I would definitely like to play for either Arsenal or Manchester United. From the time you are a small boy you want to be at the biggest club possible, and since I have had an interest in football Arsenal and United have certainly been the most successful English teams. I like to look on each move in my career as a stepping stone, and ultimately I hope that I can reach the top."
CLINTON MORRISON, BIRMINGHAM CITY'S REPUBLIC OF IRELAND STRIKER HIS CAREER ALL MAPPED OUT IF HE LEAVES ST. ANDREWS.

"I wouldn't say there's any bad things about being famous really, the attention comes with it. Sometimes it gets a little bit too much, but you've got to learn to handle that because it's part and parcel of being famous and being in a world-class team. I get a little bit more than some other people but, that's part of my life now. I've learned to handle that."
ENGLAND SKIPPER DAVID BECKHAM ON WHAT IT'S LIKE BEING ONE OF THE WORLD'S HIGHEST PROFILE PLAYERS.

"You can sometimes find having a good week of training can lead to you having a good game at the weekend. But, to be honest, I think a lot of football is played in your head. You've got to stay focussed on the job in hand and, as they say, you get out what you put in. So if you put it in during training you're likely to do well in the majority of the games you play. Rest is vital to footballers and is probably just as important as training sessions. You've got to take proper time out and put your feet up after a match."
STEVEN GERRARD REVEALS HOW HE IS ABLE TO RUN AROUND SO MUCH FOR LIVERPOOL AND ENGLAND.

PREMIERSHIP AWARDS OF THE DECADE

THE PREMIER LEAGUE CELEBRATED ITS TEN YEARS' OF EXISTENCE BY HANDING OUT VARIOUS AWARDS. A STAR-STUDDED PANEL NOMINATED THE PLAYERS AND THEN THE FANS VOTED FOR THE WINNERS. HERE ARE THE WINNERS – PLUS THE **SHOOT MONTHLY** TEAM'S OWN VERDICTS.

MATCH

A DIFFICULT ONE with so many great matches! Southampton beating Man United 6-3? It happened in season 1996-97. Bradford showed every bit of fight they had but narrowly lost to West Ham 5-4 and then there was the Leicester v Arsenal game where The Foxes managed a draw even though they probably should have won!

Who can forget White Hart Lane where Spurs had a 3-0 half-time lead over United and lost 5-3?

Game of the Decade was contested between Liverpool and Newcastle in a thrilling game that finished with The Magpies losing 4-3 in April 1996. Braces from Robbie Fowler and Stan Collymore as Kevin Keegan saw the title slipping from his grasp.

SHOOT'S VERDICT: Liverpool v Newcastle. A game that had everything: twists and turns, passion, skill, and a thrilling ending with Collymore scoring the winner. Fantastic!

GOAL

NOMINATED HERE WERE Southampton's Matt Le Tissier (twice), Dennis Bergkamp of Arsenal (twice), Tony Yeboah (Leeds), Eric Cantona (Man United), Dalian Atkinson (Aston Villa) and controversial Italian Paolo Di Canio.

But all of them were beaten by David Beckham's incredible lob from the halfway line against Wimbledon in 1996 that really put him on the path to fame. It was a great goal, unless you were unlucky goalkeeper Neil Sullivan!

SHOOT'S VERDICT: Paolo Di Canio. Who can forget his wonder volley against Wimbledon?

SAVE

THE NOMINEES INCLUDED two former West Ham keepers in Ludek Miklosko and Shaka Hislop and the present Hammers' goalie David James, then at Liverpool.

Also in the running was Kasey Keller for Leicester, Bolton's Jussi Jaaskelainen and Newcastle Republic of Ireland No.1 Shay Given. Man United's Peter Schmeichel was nominated twice and his effort against Newcastle in season 1997-98 eventually dominated the awards.

His reflex save from a powerful John Barnes header was the clear winner with 27 per cent of the votes and his other was second with 20 per cent.

SHOOT'S VERDICT: Peter Schmeichel against Newcastle. A great stop by one of the best goalkeepers ever.

PHOTOGRAPH

Impressions of Superman, punching of balls and overhead kicks here but the winning photo, taken by Phil Noble, shows everyone at Anfield in disbelief that Michael Owen didn't score. The boy's not invincible!

SHOOT'S VERDICT: Michael Owen. What a reaction by the crowd.

OVERSEAS PLAYER

ERIC CANTONA GOT YOUR VOTE but did he deserve it? The Frenchman was superb, but that karate kick on a fan at Crystal Palace was a big career let down. That said, for sheer charisma alone, King Eric was a winner.

SHOOT'S VERDICT: Gianfranco Zola. Greats such as Cantona, Bergkamp and Schmeichel were all in contention but the little Italian is at times breath-taking. His dedication to the game is amazing after such a long career and you wouldn't bet against him still playing when he soon reaches the age of 40!

DOMESTIC PLAYER

WHO ELSE BUT ALAN SHEARER? There have been many great players who have graced the Premiership with their skill and passion, but Big Al has been consistently excellent for both Blackburn and Newcastle (he played for Southampton in the old First Division). He has taken the rough with the smooth and served both club and country well.

SHOOT'S VERDICT: Ryan Giggs. He's one player who has lit up Saturday afternoons with some terrific performances. Has made being a right-back a nightmare occupation.

COMMENTATOR

WE HAVE TO LISTEN to their facts, predictions and opinions so this award is very important.

John Motson is always a favourite despite being a bit past his prime. Radio 5 Live's Alan Green is the Di Canio of radio and Mike Ingham possibly the best commentator not on screen.

You voted Martin Tyler, the voice of Sky's football coverage, the best.

SHOOT'S VERDICT: Martin Tyler. Made a brave move ten years ago by going to an unknown satellite broadcaster, but alongside Andy Gray he has become the focal point of an exciting sports' broadcasting revolution.

DOMESTIC TEAM

YOU VOTED FOR
SEAMAN
G. NEVILLE
ADAMS
BRUCE
PEARCE
BECKHAM
INCE
SCHOLES
GIGGS
OWEN
SHEARER

SHOOT'S VERDICT
SEAMAN
G. NEVILLE
ADAMS
SOUTHGATE
PEARCE
LE TISSIER
McALLISTER
SCHOLES
GIGGS
SHEARER
SHERINGHAM

David Seaman

OVERSEAS TEAM

YOU VOTED FOR
SCHMEICHEL
PETRESCU
STAM
DESAILLY
IRWIN
LJUNGBERG
VIEIRA
ROY KEANE
PIRES
HENRY
CANTONA

SHOOT'S VERDICT
SCHMEICHEL
PETRESCU
McGRATH
DESAILLY
IRWIN
LJUNGBERG
VIEIRA
ROY KEANE
GINOLA
ZOLA
HENRY

Peter Schmeichel

Gary Neville

Tony Adams

Steve Bruce

Stuart Pearce

David Beckham

Paul Ince

Paul Scholes

Ryan Giggs

Michael Owen

Alan Shearer

Dan Petrescu

Jaap Stam

Marcel Desailly

Denis Irwin

Freddie Ljungberg

Roy Keane

Patrick Vieira

Robert Pires

Thierry Henry

Eric Cantona

THE GORDON STRACHAN STORY

GORDON STRACHAN IS FAMOUS, in recent times anyway, for his television interviews. You know, those Saturday night slots on *The Premiership* that are actually more entertaining than the football itself! However, before all his interview antics, the real Gordon Strachan was a skillful and combative midfielder for Dundee, Aberdeen, Leeds, Manchester United and Scotland.

After his playing days (he carried on at the top level until he was 40!) the wee fella brought his sense of hard work and discipline into the world of management, first at Coventry City and now at Southampton. Strachan is a real motivator and is admired by many in the game. Let's take a look at the highs and lows in his amazing career.

IN THE BEGINNING

STRACHAN STARTED AT DUNDEE in 1971, before moving on to Aberdeen in 1977 for £50,000. After a slow start to his Pittodrie career he soon established himself as one of the most talented midfielders in Scotland and won the 1980 Scottish Player of the Year Award. Under the management of Alex Ferguson, Strachan and Aberdeen challenged the traditional Old Firm dominance winning Scottish Premier League titles in 1980 and 1984 and Scottish Cup Medals in 1982, 1983 and 1984. His most historic achievement during this period was when The Dons beat Real Madrid to win the Cup Winners Cup in 1983.

MOVING SOUTH

IN AUGUST 1984, the Scot joined Man United, when Ron Atkinson paid £600,000 for his services. During his time at Old Trafford, he won an FA Cup Winner's medal (left), and made 160 appearances, scoring 33 goals. Meanwhile, he was a still a regular in the Scotland side. During an international career spanning 12 years, the midfielder would go on to make 50 appearances and score five goals. His best moment came when he scored against West Germany in the 1986 World Cup. Eventually, as Alex Ferguson, by now also recruited from Aberdeen, sought to embark on a massive rebuilding programme at Old Trafford, a 32-year-old Strachan was deemed surplus to requirements and it was time to seek pastures new.

SGT. WILKO'S BARGAIN BUY

MARCH 1989... Gordon Strachan arrived at Leeds United for the bargain fee of £300,000, As captain, and club talisman, the veteran Strachan led Leeds to the old Second Division title in 1990. Then, having previously been Scottish Footballer of the Year in 1980, he became English Footballer of the Year in 1992 – the first man to win the awards both north and south of the border. To top it all off, Gordon had won the First Division Championship in the last season before the Premier League came into effect. Despite suggestions that he would be groomed to become Howard Wilkinson's successor as boss, nothing materialised and at the age of 38 he went for one last move to rejoin his former United manager, Ron Atkinson, at Coventry. With 245 appearances and some 45 goals, the whole Leeds experience was a nice way to end his playing career. Or so we thought!

MANAGEMENT BECKONS

HIS APPOINTMENT IN MARCH 1995 was supposed to be as an assistant coach but soon Coventry's annual relegation problems saw him pull on the boots once again. Still City's best player and now installed as manager (Big Ron moved "upstairs") he avoided relegation on the final day of the 1996-97 season with a nerve-wracking win at Spurs. Relative good times followed in the next campaign with Coventry building a talented squad around the likes of Dion Dublin and Darren Huckerby and the club reached the quarter-final of the FA Cup. Latterly Gary McAllister and Robbie Keane helped City stave off relegation and Strachan was hailed as one of the best young managers in the game.

RELEGATION WOE

DISASTER SOON STRUCK. The sale of Keane and McAllister allied with the failure of big signing Craig Bellamy to settle eventually saw City live up to their annual billing as relegation certainties. Coventry dropped out of the Premiership in the 2000-2001 season and after pressure from fans Gordon left the club by mutual consent weeks into the following term.

BACK ON TOP

STRACHAN BARELY HAD TIME to catch his breath before he was approached to become the new manager of Southampton who were struggling at their new stadium under rookie boss Stuart Gray. The fiery Scot soon steadied the ship and helped them to a comfortable 11th place in his first season. The 2002-03 campaign brought even more improvement, with The Saints playing free-flowing football; James Beattie banging in goals from all angles; and the club reaching the final of the FA Cup. With a UEFA Cup spot in the bag and a club on the up and up the St. Mary's faithful have a lot to look forward to – and let's not forget those hilarious post-match interviews either!

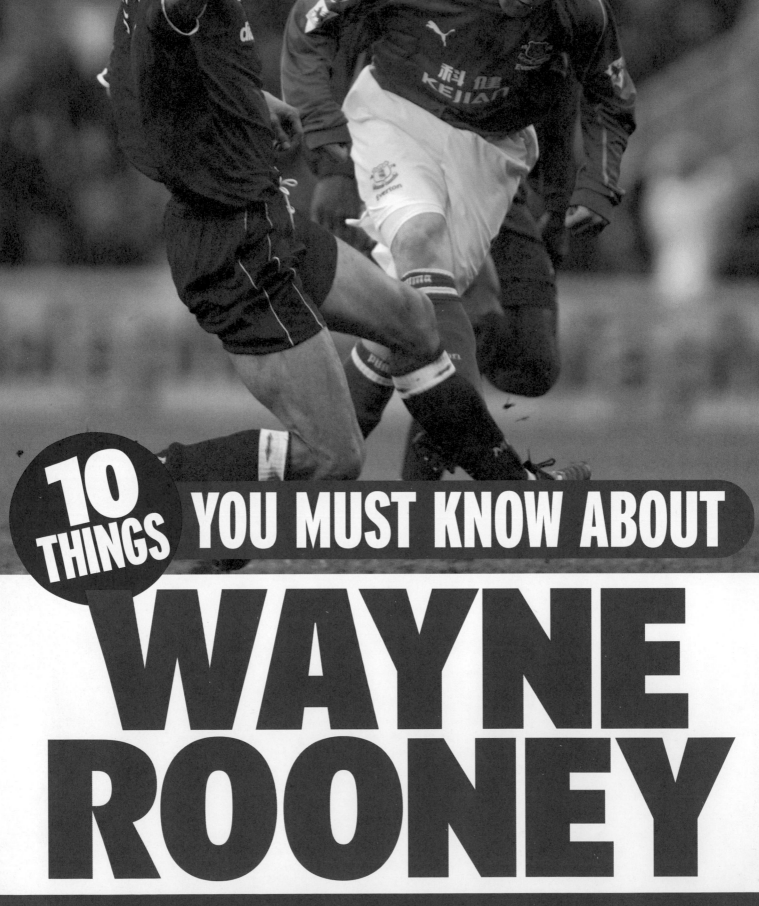

10 THINGS YOU MUST KNOW ABOUT WAYNE ROONEY

JUST WHO IS EVERTON AND ENGLAND'S WAYNE ROONEY?

1 The Everton striker was born on October 24, 1985 when Wham! were top of the pop charts with *Wake me up before you go-go.*

2 Wayne was promoted to the first-team squad last season after scoring eight goals in eight games during the previous term's FA Youth Cup. He scored a hat-trick against SC Weiz during a pre-season tour of Austria and another three against Queen's Park the following week.

3 His Premiership debut was in the 2-2 home draw with Tottenham on the opening day of 2002-03. He became Everton's youngest-ever goalscorer in the 3-0 Worthington Cup win over Wrexham.

Rooney's... the best bar none?

4 His first Premiership goal, which earned him the title of youngest-ever Premiership scorer, was in October 2002 against champions Arsenal. It earned him the Barclaycard Premiership Goal of the Month award.

5 Wayne is not The Toffees' youngest-ever player, despite making his debut at the gate of 16. That title goes to former Everton boss Joe Royle, now Ipswich manager, – but only just!

6 Wayne made nine appearances for Everton's Reserves last season but the youngster also turned out for the Under-19 side when he was only 15-years-old.

7 Wayne made his full international debut in the friendly against Australia in February 2003 and followed that with an an appearance in the Euro 2004 qualifying win against Turkey. Wayne scored a hat-trick for England last May when they beat Spain 4-1 to clinch third in the European Under-17 Championships.

8 Wayne was reportedly rejected by big rivals Liverpool, despite scoring a number of goals during a run out at The Reds' training ground when he was just nine. All of Wayne's family are true Blues and his younger brother John is also on the books at Goodison Park.

9 A Publican attempting to boost his trade has re-named his pub after the young Everton starlet. "Rooney's Bar" is situated just around the corner from Goodison Park.

10 A worried fan phoned Everton boss David Moyes to tell him he had seen young Wayne kicking a ball against a wall in a street near where he lives. The gaffer said he wasn't too concerned, because the teenager still needs to mix with his friends and try to lead a normal life.

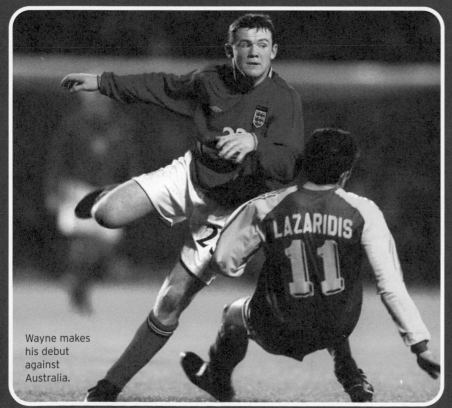

Wayne makes his debut against Australia.

DIFFICULT

TITUS BRAMBLE
CENTRE-HALF, NEWCASTLE

"I can still remember being taught a real lesson by Sunderland's Kevin Phillips when I was still at Ipswich. He was so awkward. He works on the shoulder of the last defender and makes those darting runs that are so hard to stop. He's such an intelligent player, finding space and using it against you."

JAMES BEATTIE
STRIKER, SOUTHAMPTON

"It's a toss-up between Sami Hyypia and Sol Campbell. They are both extremely fit, physical and strong in the air. And a lot of people don't realise how good they both are on the ground too. Sol is maybe a bit quicker but both never give you a minute's peace, on or off the ball."

DAYS

WE ASKED SOME TOP PREMIERSHIP STARS TO NAME THEIR NIGHTMARE OPPONENTS

MATT HOLLAND
MIDFIELD, CHARLTON ATHLETIC

"You would have to go some way to better Roy Keane. He's been an amazing player for Manchester United and Ireland. Strong in the tackle, very experienced, a real leader, anticipating everything, Roy's probably the best midfielder in Britain over the past decade. It's a shame he doesn't now play for the Republic."

PAUL SCHOLES
MIDFIELD, MAN UNITED

"When Emanuel Petit was at Arsenal I thought he was a hell of a competitor. He's obviously good now but then he was arguably at the top of his form, especially alongside Patrick Vieira. Those two could snuff out your attack and start off their own counter-attack in just a few seconds. As a midfielder you knew you were in for a tough old game."

JLLOYD SAMUEL
LEFT-BACK, ASTON VILLA

"Either Ruud Van Nistelrooy or Thierry Henry. They are very different players – Van Nistelrooy is deadly in the box, very quick to react to situations and can score with either foot. Henry plays more outside the box, has amazing pace and can pull out wide to create chances for others. They're both excellent and no, I won't say who I think is the best!"

REACH FOR THE SKY

SATELLITE BROADCASTER SKY SPORTS HAS REVOLUTIONISED THE WAY WE WATCH FOOTBALL, SHOWING EVERY COMPETITION FROM INTERNATIONALS, THE PREMIERSHIP, NATIONWIDE GAMES DOWN TO THE CONFERENCE AND MAJOR OVERSEAS FIXTURES. BUT WHAT HAPPENS BEHIND THE SCENES?

SOCCER AM

PRESENTERS: Helen Chamberlain and Tim Lovejoy.
WHAT'S IT ABOUT?: The three-hour long Saturday morning football magazine programme includes fans in the studio, guest footballers and celebrity fans. Chelsea fan Tim is unique at Sky in that he is both producer and presenter. Helen supports Torquay United (well someone has to!).
What's your most memorable moment on the show?
HELEN: "When Robbie Fowler revealed that his middle name was Bernard!"
TIM: "Beating Paul Gascoigne at table tennis live on air."
How much preparation do you have to do before going on air?
H: "I just come in on Thursday, Friday and Saturday!"
T: "Including the live show the crew works six days a week ten months a year."
Do you dash straight off to see games when you get off air?
H: "It's not uncommon for me to tear off to Torquay and beyond after the show and I often make it for kick-off too!"
T: "I go to most Chelsea home games, and it's only half an hour away."
Who are your favourite footballers past and present?
H: "Rodney Jack (past) and Tony Bedeau (present)."
T: "Probably Kerry Dixon (past) and Gianfranco Zola (present)."
DID YOU KNOW? Tim used to be a researcher and then producer of *The Big Breakfast*. Helen began her career as a Blue Coat at Pontins.

The Soccer Saturday team prepare to go on-air.

Jeff Stelling holds things together for an amazing five and a half hours

There's never a quiet moment on Sky's Saturday morning funfest.

SOCCER SATURDAY

PRESENTER: Jeff Stelling **GUEST PANEL:** George Best, Rodney Marsh, Frank McLintock, Tony Cottee and others.
WHAT'S IT ABOUT? If you can't get to the game *Soccer Saturday* has become vital viewing on a Saturday afternoon thanks to Jeff and his panel. Amazingly, Jeff manages to hold the live programme together for five and a half hours and keep it interesting, even when there are no scores coming through.
How much preparation do you do for the programme?
"I do much of it on the Friday, more or less a full day, sometimes up to about 9pm."
Do you sit there for the full show – or do you nip to the toilet or for a quick drink?
"We're lucky enough to have food and drink brought to us but I make the odd dash to the loo – it's a long show!"
How do you put up with Rodney Marsh's sometimes off-beat and cutting comments?
"After all these years I've developed a thick skin!"
Who are your favourite footballers past and present?
"Alan Shearer's a superb professional in every way, and Rodney Marsh was my boyhood hero."
DID YOU KNOW? Jeff Stelling is a Hartlepool United fan who started his journalism career on a local newspaper and radio station.

Behind the scenes on match-day.

SUPER SUNDAY

PRESENTER: Richards Keys
GUESTS: Varied, including Alan Shearer and Graeme Souness.
WHAT'S IT ABOUT? Pre-match analysis and full match coverage from a top Premier League fixture.

Richard, don't you ever get tired of seeing so much football?
"Not at all, I've always felt it was a real privilege to do what I do."

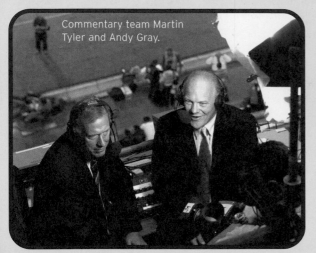
Commentary team Martin Tyler and Andy Gray.

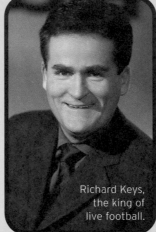
Richard Keys, the king of live football.

Do you talk football when you meet up with friends away from work?
"Of course! I've always been a fan first and foremost."

What's the biggest clanger you have dropped on live television?
"As we were going into the second-half of a Sheffield United v Coventry City game (it was 0-0) I said: 'This one's got goals written all over it.' The second-half was even worse than a turgid first 45 minutes and finished 0-0."

Who are your favourite footballers past and present?
"Alan Shearer (present) and Gary McAllister when at Coventry (past)."

DID YOU KNOW? Richard has presented more live football than any other British broadcaster, including Sky's first live game, the Rangers v Dundee United match in April 1991.

MONDAY NIGHT FOOTBALL

PRESENTERS: Ian Payne and Andy Gray. Richard Keys was the anchorman until this season.

WHAT'S IT ABOUT? Pre-match analysis and coverage from a top Premiership game.

Ian, you made a good name for yourself on radio, why the switch to television?
"I've always wanted to do TV - presenting football is every fan/broadcaster's dream - and to join the guys with all the football seemed the right move."

Is television any more difficult than radio?
"I'll let you know in a year or so!"

What was your most embarrassing radio moment?
"When we called English radio personality Tommy Boyd by mistake, when we thought the Scotland international of the same name would give us his thoughts on a Euro '96 match! It was a live interview that soon became highly embarrassing!"

Who are your favourite footballers past and present?
"Leeds United's Johnny Giles (past) and Zinedine Zidane (present)."

Do you remember the first live football game you attended?
"Yes, I went to see Oxford United v Bournemouth in 1975."

DID YOU KNOW? Former PFA Player of the Year Andy was actually assistant boss at one of his former clubs, Aston Villa.

Andy and Richard Keys go through their pre-match analysis.

Ian Payne

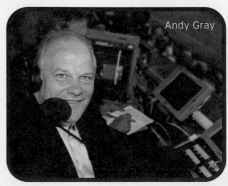
Andy Gray

48

FRANKLY SPEAKING

SKY PUNDIT FRANK McLINTOCK CAN TALK WITH REAL AUTHORITY HAVING PLAYED AND MANAGED AT THE HIGHEST LEVEL. WE GAVE HIM SIX TOUGH QUESTIONS.

HOW HAS FOOTBALL CHANGED SINCE YOUR DAY?

"I think the game has got quicker. I think there's a little bit more skill involved as well, partly because of the amount of foreign players that have been brought in. Obviously the money factor is the biggest change of all. It's really quite unbelievable to guys of my age when we were on about £100 a week - we started on £20 a week. My best wages were at QPR at the end of my career and that was £200 a week basic."

DO YOU BEGRUDGE WHAT THE MODERN-DAY FOOTBALLER EARNS?

"I have said for years on TV that I think it's wrong. I think it's gone too far. Clubs can't afford to pay the wages that have been paid in the past five, six, seven years. I think players get almost spoiled and think they are better than what they are at the age of 22 when they've got £4m or £5m in the bank. A lot of them will lose their ambition and drive and discipline."

DO YOU FEEL FOREIGN PLAYERS HAVE BEEN GOOD FOR THE ENGLISH GAME?

"Overall there's an awful lot of good players. People like Dennis Bergkamp - one of the best players Arsenal have ever had - Thierry Henry and Patrick Vieira. Then you've got Gianfranco Zola who's a magnificent professional and everybody loves him. Eric Cantona coming on the scene, I really did think he was fantastic. But they've also brought tumbling over in the 18-yard box all the time, which I really dislike. It annoys me when I see them rolling about in agony. Watch a rugby match and you see players getting stamped on the head but they get up and get on with it."

WHAT DID IT MEAN TO YOU TO CAPTAIN ARSENAL TO THE LEAGUE AND FA CUP DOUBLE IN 1971?

"It was fantastic. I suppose I was a sort of natural leader. Even at 19 I was shouting and praising people, patting them on the back and kicking them up the bum, even though I had just walked into the first-team. I had great passion for the game."

CAN YOU COMPARE YOUR ARSENAL TEAM AND THE CURRENT SIDE?

"I think it was harder in our day to win the Double than it was for Arsene Wenger's team. That's not taking anything away from them, but they can handpick players from all over the world, whereas we had more or less 13 players that won the Double. I love the football that they play, there's no jealousy, but I do think they lack a little bit of meanness."

IN YOUR OPINION WHAT'S THE BEST LEAGUE IN EUROPE?

"I think for excitement and for all-round ability, the Premier league. Whether a team's at the bottom or at the top they will fight right to the end. But if you're talking about real class I would say the Spanish league has got better quality players and play fractionally more attractive football with fractionally higher skill levels."

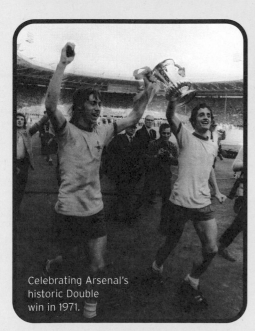

Celebrating Arsenal's historic Double win in 1971.

WEB

NOTHING CAN BEAT GOING TO A GAME BUT IF YOU ARE STUCK AT HOME AND NEED FOOTBALL, TRY SURFING THE NET

UNOFFICIAL MAGPIES
● www.nufc.com

THIS SITE IS A source of annoyance to the club as, despite its dot.com status it is unofficial. Newcastle have evidently tried to buy the site. There are plenty of good stories here, much light-hearted humour and some stinging criticisms when the club gets it wrong. To be admired for being kept as up-to-date as possible.

RED NEWS
● www.rednews.co.uk

CLAIMED TO HAVE begun life in 1987 - surely not on The Net? - from the occasional checks we made on this site it does at least appear to update its news content regularly. There are also a number of Manchester United features, a European section and the now almost compulsory shopping pages. They claim to be the first United fanzine, but there are thousands more now on the Web.

THIS IS ANFIELD
● www.thisisanfield.com

YOU MIGHT HAVE to look twice at this site, just to confirm that it is not an official one from the club. There are regular news updates, features written by a number of obviously dedicated fans, match reports, a fans' forum, player biogs, fixtures and even a regular chance to vote on Anfield happenings. Nicely presented too.

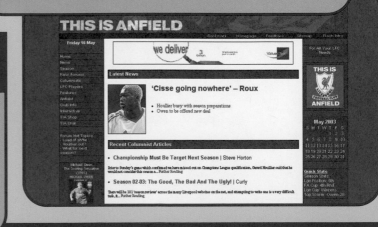

GOONER LIKE IT
● www.onlinegooner.com

YOU GUESSED, an Arsenal fanzine! News and features, opinions, all expressed in a way only a true fan could, and the chance to give your ideas and vote on happenings at Highbury. There are a few digs at Manchester United, as you would expect, and an archive section just in case you need something to read when there's no football being played. Heavy on words, but still quality.

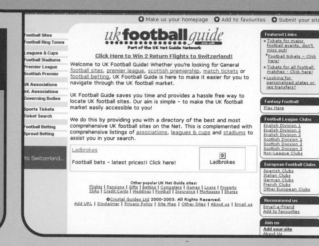

THE FOOTBALL GUIDE
● www.ukfootballguide.co.uk

LOTS OF WEBSITES are there one minute and gone the next, so something like this can be invaluable. It's exactly what it says on the screen, a guide to some of the best (and a few of the worst!) football websites currently on the Internet. There are also a number of links to official bodies and a few sites trying to sell you things, like ringtones.

BLUE KIPPER
● www.bluekipper.com

EVEN IF YOU ARE NOT an Everton fan you will probably be able to laugh at the Scouse humour on this great site. Put together by "a gang of Evertonians who have known each other for 25 years" it offers both entertainment and information. They even got Wayne Rooney to say a few words and hold up one of their t-shirts - now there's a vote of confidence. Updated regularly.

NOT A MISPRINT...
● www.manchestreunited.com

WE HAVE SPELT the name of this site correctly! Type it in as it is, because these pages are aimed at taking the mickey out of everyone's favourite hate team (well, except their own fans) Manchester United. As it points out, it is "not intended to offend" but wants to give an alternative and humourous view, even if sometimes it is cutting.

DOWN BY THE RIVER
● www.borobarmy.com

THIS REALLY IS a good site if you are a Middlesbrough fan or want to know more about what is going on at The Riverside. Ticket details, player fact files, results... it has the lot here. Well, almost! There were a few gaps in the information we looked at but, to be honest, the rest of the stuff on here makes it a worthwhile visit. There was even good info on England's visit during 2003.

WEB

FLYING THE FLAG
● www.the-fa.org

PROBABLY YOUR FIRST point of call for any England international information, on all teams from the teenage side right up to the full senior squad. Stats, latest squads, results, FA Cup and the women's game all get coverage. But if you are involved in grassroots or children's football it's also worth a visit to get the latest lowdown.

THINKING FANS
● www.footie51.co.uk

THIS IS A SORT OF grown-up fanzine website, and it's pretty good. They don't go for the usual results, best players, stats routine here, but offer up a selection of decent features covering many aspects of football, particularly in Britain. Anything from finance to hooliganism could be covered here, along with book reviews and their Beginners Guides to... which cover lots of different things.

FROM THE OTHER SIDE
● www.englishfootball.com

IF YOU WANT something other than the official view of all matters England then this is a site to try out. It isn't always totally up-to-date, but it is interesting to see how the thoughts of other fans of the national side compare to yours. There's also a history section, links to a page on all the major clubs plus a star of the month feature.

GREAT GOODIES
● www.bid4sport.com

FORMER LIVERPOOL, NEWCASTLE and Sunderland player Barry Venison set up this site where you can get hold of lots of rather special sporting items, and not just from famous football stars. There are lots of signed goodies up for auction, and the profits are donated to special charities. So not only could you grab a piece of history, but you can also help those more needy.

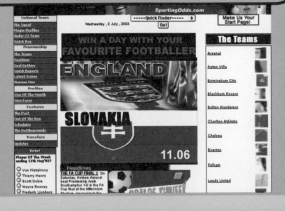

WATCH

A DIFFERENT GAME
• www.4-3-3.com

THE ADDRESS FOR this site is obviously a play on the slightly more usual team formation of 4-4-2, and if you visit you can probably see why. Basically this is your chance to play a football game which is also slightly different. You have to earn promotion from the basement divisions to the top flight - and they stop you from cheating! You even get attendance figures to go with results.

YOUR DAILY HELPING
• www.skysports.com

OUR FRIENDS AT Sky offer you loads of information and stats on various sports, but there's more than enough football here. There are also columns from some of their star names, like pundit Andy Gray; sections for every major side in the country; plus the latest team news and transfers. Great if you can't get to the teletext.

...DON'T FORGET US!
• www.shoot.co.uk

YOU'VE BOUGHT THE annual, hopefully you buy the monthly version too - and now you can also check out the Shoot Monthly website. We'll let you know the major news stories as they happen, you can check out how to get back numbers, there's a sneak preview before each edition hits the streets, plus the chance to play free fantasy football.

WORLD-BEATERS
• www.worldsoccer.com

AS OUR SISTER magazine, World Soccer brings you the best of what is happening right around the globe in the great game of football. But if you can't wait a month between editions you can log on to their website and find the latest scores and news, all updated on a regular basis. There are also a number of links to other sites if you just can't get enough of football in this country.

TRADING

MICKY ADAMS

Did his Mam cut cut his hair when he played at Coventry? Looks like Leicester boss Micky Adams has now got himself a proper barber.

DAVID O'LEARY

From silverware at Arsenal to silver hair at Aston Villa, but David O'Leary has generally aged well. Shame about the mad stare!

ARSENE WENGER

Even during his early coaching career, Arsene Wenger always sported the look of a French professor. Graduation from Monaco to Arsenal has been achieved with top marks.

HARRY REDKNAPP

Harry boy obviously enjoys the South Coast air. From his early managerial days at Bournemouth, he has settled once again near the Channel with Premiership new boys Portsmouth.

FACES

BAD HAIRCUTS, EVEN WORST FACIAL HAIR - LOOK AT HOW THE YEARS HAVE AFFECTED SOME OF THE BIGGEST NAMES IN FOOTBALL.

SAM ALLARDYCE

In his playing days at Sunderland he looked like actor Tom Selleck, TV detective Magnum. Now, he fires Magnums in Bolton's dressing room.

ANDY GRAY

Clearly a case of hair today, gone tomorrow for Sky's expert summariser. In his day he was the best header of a football in the game. Unfortunately for Andy, it appears to have worn away the thatch a bit too much.

GRAEME SOUNESS

It is difficult to believe that Tottenham sold Graeme Souness as a youngster to Boro. A successful career as player and manager followed, as did several wild hairstyles.

MARK HUGHES

Twenty years ago he led the line for Manchester United, now Sparky is looking forward to leading Wales into European Championship action in Portugal next Summer.

CRAZY?

CLUES ACROSS

1. Dario, boss who led Crewe back to Division One (5)
4. Manager of First Division champions, Pompey (8)
8. Chris, former Blackburn Rovers and Chelsea striker in Celtic's UEFA Cup squad (6)
9. Young forward, James, who broke into the Leeds United side last term (6)
11. See 16 Down
12. Swedish striker, Marcus, on target for Villa in 2003 (7)
13. Fabian, Surinam-born Dutch defender in England with Ipswich Town (6)
15. Fulham and France forward, Steve (6)
18. Blackburn Rovers star, Matt, whose career survived a serious car accident (6)
19. - - - Orient, the Os from the Matchroom Stadium, Brisbane Road (6)
22. Nickname associated with 2. Down (7)
24. Nationality of Bayern Munich's Owen Hargreaves (7)
27. Covered passageway leading from pitch to dressing rooms (6)
28. Laurent, French winger in Newcastle's Champions League squad (6)
29. Manager whose club won the 2003 Worthington Cup in Cardiff (8)
30. Charlton's former Bury goalkeeper, Dean (5)

CLUES DOWN

1. - - - Crooks, former Tottenham Hotspur striker, now a TV soccer interviewer (5)
2. Southampton's 2003 FA Cup Final opponents (7)
3. Local rivals that met AC Milan in the Champions League semi-final (5)
4. Teenage Everton sensation who made his full senior England debut last season (6)
5. Aussie full-back, Lucas, at Ewood Park (5)
6. Highbury's England Under-21 midfielder, Jermaine (7)
7. England's Swedish coach (8)
10. Country which staged the 2002 World Cup Final (5)
13. The Magpies' former Leeds United centre-back, Jonathan (8)
14. - - - Walker, keeper who helped Leicester back into the Premiership (3)
16. and 11. Across Birmingham-born Aston Villa and England midfielder (3, 7)
17. Craig Bellamy's nationality (5)
18. Brazilian midfield star who returned to The Riverside Stadium last year (7)
20. Partick or Inverness Caledonian (7)
21. Rangers' Dutch defender, Ronald (2,4)
23. Former Dons striker, Jason, now at The Valley (5)
25. Nationality of Nikos Dabizas (5)
26. England's Footballer of the Year, 2003 (5)

GOAL GRABBER 2

DATE: May 28, 2003
VENUE: South Africa
MATCH: South Africa v England
RESULT: 1-2
Name the goalscorer from the players listed below:
A. Emile Heskey
B. Gareth Southgate
C. Matthew Upson
D. Michael Owen

QUICK QUIZ 2

1. Which club plays at the Withdean Stadium?
2. In which year did Coventry City win the FA Cup for the only time in their history?
3. Who did Rangers defeat in last season's Scottish FA Cup Final?
4. Who are the current champions in Italy?
5. Ron Atkinson, Ossie Ardiles and Bobby Gould have all managed this club. Name the side.
6. What nationality is Manchester United player Quinton Fortune?
7. Graham Poll, Paul Durkin and Andy D'Urso are all what?
8. Which team lost in both the semi-finals of the Worthington Cup and FA Cup last season?
9. Which Arsenal boss brought Dennis Bergkamp (right) to Highbury?
10. Name the two Nationwide League clubs in the county of Devon.

WHO AM I?

See if you can identify this player from the clues below.
1. I began my career at Highbury.
2. I played for Bristol City and Fulham before moving to the North East.
3. I was voted PFA Young Player of the Year in 1994.
4. I hit the bar with a header on my England debut but have only scored once for my country.
5. I helped win the 2002 Worthington Cup Final.

SEE ANSWERS PAGE 111

THE REASONS BECKS
WANTS TO REIGN IN SPAIN

WHAT WAS THE REAL DEAL OVER DAVID BECKHAM'S MOVE TO MADRID? WE GIVE YOU SOME STRAIGHT ANSWERS.

WHY DID HE HAVE TO LEAVE MANCHESTER UNITED?

Quite simply, it was probably now or never. At the age of 28 Becks is still in his prime, but with his contract fast running out at Old Trafford he would be worth very little on the transfer market in a few years' time. Oh and maybe it had something to do with Fergie...

SO DID THE FACT THAT HIS MANAGER KICKED A BOOT AT HIM HAVE ANY INFLUENCE ON BECKS LEAVING?

Well, we're not quite sure whether the boot was actually meant to hit Becks, but there is no doubt that it didn't help his relationship with Sir Alex Ferguson. There was already a sort of uneasy truce between them. Both admit total respect for each other's ability, but the boss wasn't too keen on the jet-set lifestyle of the Beckhams or some of David's tastes in fashion and clothes.

ALL SORTS OF CLUBS WERE LINKED WITH A MOVE FOR HIM, WAS THERE ANY TRUTH IN THE RUMOURS?

The likes of Barcelona and both Milan clubs could possibly have wanted the

England skipper in their sides but the only buyer was ever going to be Real Madrid. With respect, Inter and AC are probably not as big as United, and Barca couldn't offer him European football, a must. Also, Real meant he had the chance of playing with some of the world's best players, like Zinedine Zidane.

WAS £25m A GOOD PRICE? SHOULDN'T HE HAVE COST MADRID A LOT MORE AS HE WAS SAID TO BE WORTH £40m JUST A YEAR AGO?

It was a pretty good deal all round. United couldn't expect much more as transfer fees have slumped dramatically and without having the player on a long-term contact that also meant his value was lower. In fact, Real would have got him even cheaper if it wasn't for the fact that they can probably make loads of money selling Beckham shirts and branded products.

SO WHAT WILL BECKS GET FROM THE MOVE?

He'll have got himself a nice big pay rise and a share of the transfer fee as he did not ask for the move. However, it won't be that clear cut. David has got some of the best advisors in the game and there will be all sorts of deals and clauses in his contract. These will probably include win bonuses, appearance money, European and domestic success and a share of any money that comes in as a direct result of using his name. Let's put it this way, he'll be able to afford a few new hair bands. Football-wise it should be the perfect finishing school for his talents.

WILL HE BE ABLE TO BUY A MASSIVE HOUSE IN SPAIN?

More than likely he'll live in a very select suburb of the city, an exclusive area which is already home to many of Real's big-name overseas stars, such as Ronaldo. He'll probably rub shoulders with actors and film stars and the exact location will probably be kept as secret as possible.

WILL HE HAVE TO LEARN THE LANGUAGE?

This is a must! His team-mates won't talk to him half as much if he can't speak the same lingo – although people like Roberto Carlos are pretty fluent in English. Learning Spanish will also gain him a lot of respect with the fans and particularly the media if he can answer them in their native tongue. At his press conference he managed a pretty good "gracias."

THERE WAS TALK HE COULD COME BACK TO ENGLAND AND PLAY FOR ARSENAL IF THE MOVE GOES PEAR-SHAPED. SURELY NOT?

It could happen. Remember that he is a London boy, and if Arsenal are still challenging for honours – which they probably will be – he might like to try his chances with another team. The Gunners have a pretty strict wage policy so he would probably have to take a pay cut, but at least he would be able to live at his Hertfordshire mansion, which he won't be selling despite his move overseas.

10 FACTS ABOUT BECKS

- He was born in Leytonstone, East London on May 2, 1975.
- Made his Manchester United senior debut against Brighton, coming on as a substitute in September 1992.
- He was said to be the Most Valuable Player and best midfielder in the 1999 UEFA awards. He was voted BBC Sports Personality of the Year and came second in the FIFA World Player of the Year poll, both in 2001.
- He married Victoria Adams, Posh Spice, on July 4, 1999, at a castle near Dublin.
- Not surprisingly his dream is to have a World Cup winner's medal.
- David wears a new pair of adidas football boots for every major game he plays at an estimated cost of £300 a pair. Each have his childrens' names stitched into them.
- If he had not been a footballer, David said he might have enjoyed being a cricketer.
- His best friend is England and Man United defender Gary Neville, who was best man at his wedding
- Beckham announced his arrival with a 57-yard goal scored from near the

A FRESH START David and his pop star wife Victoria will be the celebrities of Madrid

60

TALKING FOOTBALL...

HERE ARE SOME OF THE THINGS DAVID BECKHAM HAS TOLD **SHOOT** OVER THE PAST FEW YEARS.

"It's every player's dream to play for England, let alone captain the team. I'm not one of those captains who shouts and has a go at players unless I need to. But hopefully I'm someone the players can look to if a game's not going our way."

"I don't think you can ever say that you're definitely going to stay in one place, but as long as I'm happy at Man United and they're happy with me, that's where I'll carry on playing, enjoying my football and hopefully winning even more trophies."

"I have had so many highlights, so many with the team (England) and a few on my own. I think coming second best in the world awards was something special for me and winning the treble (with Man United) is something that I'll always cherish."

ON YER HEAD SON From an early age Brooklyn was a big Manchester United fan

half-way line against Wimbledon in the opening fixture of 1996-1997.
• David has his two sons' names tattooed on his back. Brooklyn's name is on his lower back and Romeo's is on the back of his shoulders. Wife Victoria's name is tattooed (although mis-spelled) in Hindi on his arm.

"Playing at Old Trafford is a special thing for most players, but I absolutely love it because I am a fan as well. I don't feel any pressure, it's just a pleasure being involved with Manchester United and to walk out there with the team. We've got something special here. It's a dream come true, it's something that I've always wanted to do and something that I have succeeded in doing,"

"You're always going to get world-class players standing out - the Zidanes (right), Rivaldos, Figos, Carlos'. Players like that are always going to be class."

"I wouldn't say there's any bad things about being famous really. Sometimes it gets a little bit too much, but you've got to learn to handle that because it's part and parcel of being famous and being in a world-class football team. I get a little bit more than some other people but, that's part of my life now. I've learned to handle that."

TAILOR-MADE Becks has the names of his sons Brooklyn and Romeo stitched into his boots

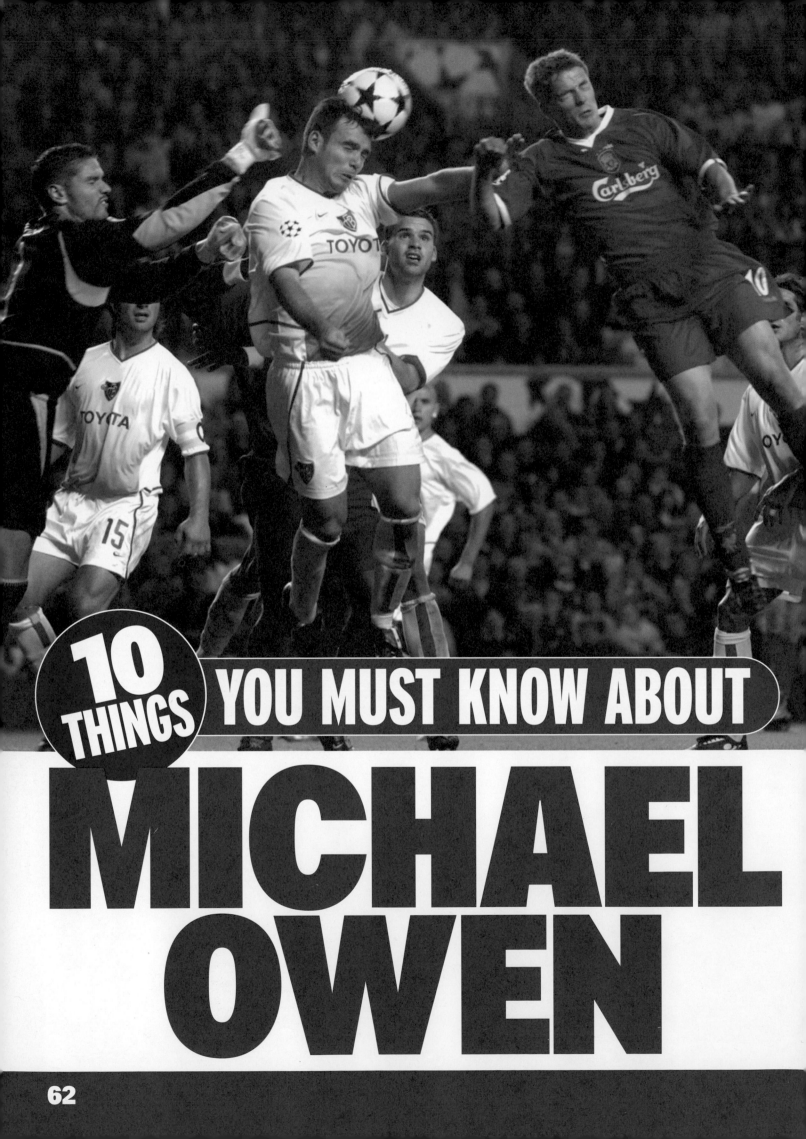

10 THINGS YOU MUST KNOW ABOUT MICHAEL OWEN

JUST WHO IS THE LIVERPOOL AND ENGLAND STRIKER?

1 He was born Michael James Owen on December 14, 1979 in Chester. The debate still rages that because he was brought up on the England-Wales border that he might play for the Welsh. Thankfully for Sven's boys he elected to play for his country of birth.

2 He has two brothers (Andrew and Terry) and two sisters (Karen and Lesley). He still keeps his home in Hawarden, Flintshire and famously bought a street full of houses for his family to live in. Mind you, he can afford it – he is currently said to earn £6.2m a year!

3 A keen student he managed to pass an impressive ten GCSEs while still pursuing a career in football. He's also a bit good at playing golf!

4 Football is in Michael's blood as his father Terry, still a keen follower of his son's career, played for both Chester City, where his picture hangs in the boardroom, and Everton.

5 The Liverpool man recently became a father for the first time when his childhood sweetheart Louise Bonsall gave birth to a baby girl named Gemma Rose.

5 Even as a youngster, Michael was a record-breaker. At the age of 11 he went past Ian Rush's record – set 20 years earlier – when he scored 79 goals for Deeside Primary School.

6 Liverpool fought off Chelsea, Manchester United and Michael's favourite side Everton to secure his services. His first job was as a YTS apprentice earning just £42.50 a week.

Michael with his European Player of the Year award in 1991.

7 It wasn't long before he had the happy knack of finding the net on his first appearance at every level played. His first senior goal against Wimbledon in 1997 followed on from debut strikes for youth and reserve teams, England schoolboys and England Under-21s. He has since gone on to score more than 100 Premier League goals, making him one of only ten players to reach that landmark in the top-flight. He's on target to be England's No.1 scorer.

8 In February 1998 Michael became the youngest player of the 20th century to represent England - less than two years after winning the FA Youth Cup for Liverpool. He scored the goal of the tournament against Argentina at the 1998 World Cup Finals. He has now scored more goals for England than any other Liverpool player and having collected 50 caps could even end up as his country's No.1 for appearances made.

9 He was awarded the Young Player Of The Year award in both 1998 and 1999 and picked up the 2001 European Footballer of the Year accolade.

10 His much-publicised love of a gamble is demonstrated by him owning a number of race horses and a box at Chester. Aside from racing he lists among his pastimes music, naming The Lightning Seeds as one of his favourite bands!

Michael scores his 1998 World Cup goal against Argentina.

WE WILL FOLLOW....

HERE ARE SOME OF THE FAMOUS NAMES WHO FOLLOW THE COUNTRY'S TOP FOOTBALL SIDES - OR AT LEAST THAT IS WHAT WE BELIEVE!

RALF LITTLE
TV's Royle Family
MANCHESTER UNITED

"When I was at school everybody supported Liverpool because they were the top team at the time. When I told my uncle that I supported Liverpool too, he gave me a real telling off and I've supported United ever since. Mark Hughes was such a quality player and he always did so much for the team. He's the player I try and model my own game on because he really was a top striker and brilliant player for United."

PREMIERSHIP SIDES' FAMOUS FANS

ARSENAL
Jockey Frankie Dettori

ASTON VILLA
Tory boss Iain Duncan Smith (left)
BIRMINGHAM
Comedian Jasper Carrott (left)
BLACKBURN
Former Superbike champion Carl Fogarty
BOLTON Comedian Peter Kay (the John Smith's adverts!)
CHARLTON
TV celebrity Jim Davidson (left)
CHELSEA
Actor Michael Caine (left)
EVERTON
England rugby star Austin Healey

ANT AND DEC
TV presenters
NEWCASTLE UNITED

ANT: "I wasn't actually allowed to go to a match until I was about 13 because of the football violence! My first match was against Grimsby when we were in the First Division when Jim Smith was the manager. After that I spent all my pocket money on going to games."

DEC: "Peter Beardsley (right) is our favourite player. He's one of the nicest blokes you could ever meet, as well as being the ultimate pro. Me and Dec have been lucky enough to play with him a few times and he's a good friend of ours now."

JONATHAN PEARCE
BBC Radio Five Commentator
BRISTOL CITY

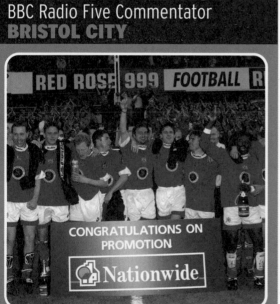

RED ROSE 999 FOOTBALL

CONGRATULATIONS ON PROMOTION
Nationwide

"I moved to Bristol when I was seven and first went to see them play with my Dad. He became the youth education officer and he used to video all the games for training purposes. I later trained with the club as a schoolboy. The night of our promotion to the First Division was a truly unforgettable night."

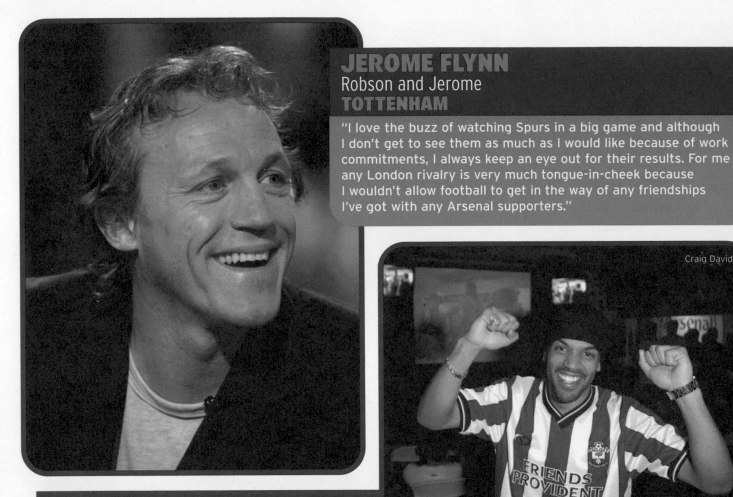

JEROME FLYNN
Robson and Jerome
TOTTENHAM

"I love the buzz of watching Spurs in a big game and although I don't get to see them as much as I would like because of work commitments, I always keep an eye out for their results. For me any London rivalry is very much tongue-in-cheek because I wouldn't allow football to get in the way of any friendships I've got with any Arsenal supporters."

Craig David

FULHAM Actor Hugh Grant
LEEDS England cricketer Nasser Hussain
LEICESTER Actor David Neilson (Roy Cropper Coronation Street)
LIVERPOOL Sporty Spice Mel C
MAN CITY Bruce Jones (Les Battersby Coronation Street)
MAN UNITED Simply Red's Mick Hucknall
MIDDLESBROUGH Singer Chris Rea
NEWCASTLE Actor and singer Jimmy Nail (Auf Weidershen Pet)
PORTSMOUTH Radio presenter Tommy Boyd (Talk Sport)
SOUTHAMPTON r and b singer Craig David
TOTTENHAM singer Phil Collins (Genesis)
WOLVES Rock star Robert Plant (Led Zeppelin)

Hugh Grant

Mel C

Mick Hucknall

Robert Plant

AND LOWER DOWN THE SCALE

BARNSLEY
TV interviewer Michael Parkinson
BRIGHTON
Norman Cook (DJ Fat Boy Slim)
DARLINGTON
Comedian Vic Reeves
NOTTINGHAM FOREST
Singer James Dean Bradfield (Manic Street Preachers)
QPR Actor Martin Clunes (Men Behaving Badly)
SHEFFIELD UNITED
Rock star Joe Elliott (Def Leppard)
SHEFFIELD WEDNESDAY
Roy Hattersley (former deputy leader Labour Party)
TRANMERE
TV presenter Ray Stubbs (BBC Football Focus)
WATFORD Singer Geri Halliwell (Spice Girl)
WOKING Martin Tyler, (Sky Sports football presenter)

OUR HEROES!

We've all got our favourite players. Strikers who always hit the back of the net. Midfielders who split defences with pin-point passes. Defenders who dish out hard but fair ball-winning tackles. Or keepers who can fly through the air like superman. Check out some of the biggest names from your Premiership club...

ARSENAL HERO
PATRICK VIEIRA

BORN: June 23, 1976, Dakar.
HEIGHT: 6ft 4in
CLUBS: Cannes, AC Milan.
WHY DO THEY LIKE HIM?
Strong, resilient, committed,
the total midfield general.

TOP GUNNERS
ARSENAL

A LOOK THROUGH the history of Arsenal reveals so many big-names players that it is difficult to pick out just a few. George Graham made his name at the North London club both as a player and manager; Liam Brady was the Irishman they thought they would never be able to replace in midfield; Charlie George the long-haired striker who also made front page headlines with his playboy lifestyle.

Scotland striker Charlie Nicholas, now a TV pundit, had the trickery to get fans on the edge of their seats and, of course, let's not forget pony-tailed David Seaman who was at the club during the careers of many great players. The England keeper will probably be remembered best as being part of that famous back five that beat all-comers: Seaman, Lee Dixon, Nigel Winterburn, Tony Adams and Martin Keown. Will they ever be replaced? And let's not forget French manager Arsene Wenger.

Above: David Seaman will never be forgotten at Highbury.
Right: George Graham collected trophies as a boss after a great career.

HEROES PAST

WITH SO MANY star Gunners to choose from it's difficult to pinpoint just two names, but we went for former skipper **TONY ADAMS** (1983-2002) and record scorer **IAN WRIGHT** (1991-98).

These two players represent the best attitudes that you will find with all of the club's star players: sheer determination and total dedication to the cause.

Big Tony might have had off-the-field problems but when it came to the team-sheet his would be the first on it, for club and country.

Wrighty hit 128 goals for The Gunners and he was the player your club wouldn't want to face!

HEROES PRESENT

THERE ARE A NUMBER of heroes at Highbury thanks to boss Arsene Wenger but we go for one at each end of the pitch : France striker **THIERRY HENRY** and England defender **SOL CAMPBELL**.

Thierry is sheer class and has been called one of the best players on the planet by former Gunner Frank McLintock. His goals grab the headlines but his speed and skill are both awesome.

Sol is the rock on which the club won its League and FA Cup Double in 2002 following his controversial move from big rivals Spurs. Since then the big man has got better as his confidence has grown.

HEROES FUTURE

YOUNG PLAYERS coming through the ranks in North London have found it difficult to break into the first-team in recent years, but England defender **ASHLEY COLE** is a big exception to that rule.

Given his chance a few years ago he grabbed it with both feet and only injuries and suspension have held him back. He's working on the disciplinary side of his game!

Another youngster you can expect to see more of is another left-footed defender, **RYAN GARRY**, who arrived in the senior squad last season.

An Essex lad, he is determined to prove himself at Arsenal.

MAJOR VILLANS
ASTON VILLA

ASTON VILLA were the undisputed kings of England's second city until rivals Birmingham got promotion to the Premiership. But that only told half the story as Villa hadn't really lived up to the their big name status or the fans' dreams for years.

In truth, it was the names of past heroes that kept many of them going. David Platt, Dwight Yorke, manager Big Ron Atkinson, Paul McGrath and a whole host of others have passed through the Villa Park gates.

They won the old First Division in 1980-81 under Ron Saunders but since then life hasn't always been sweet.

There have been the occasional signs that the club could bounce back to its former glory days but inconsistency has cost them dear.

Many big name bosses have tried and failed - including former England manager Graham Taylor and John Gregory - now ex-Leeds chief David O'Leary has a chance.

Above: David Platt starred before going to Italy.
Left: Dwight Yorke's goals earned him a move to Man United.

HEROES PAST

ANDY GRAY, yes it's the same one you now see on Sky Sports, giving informed comments about games. He made his name at Villa (1975-79; 1985-87), Wolves, Everton and Scotland. Those were the days when they had heroes to admire north of the Border. Later returned to Villa as assistant boss but has proved he is as talented on television as he was playing.

PETER WITHE (1980-85) also played for Nottingham Forest and Newcastle, but it was his goal that made Villa Champions of Europe that earned him cult status. Good on the deck, he was also a super header of the ball and had no fear.

HEROES PRESENT

DION DUBLIN began his Villa career in 1998 after playing for Cambridge, Man United and Coventry. He's proved more than useful at centre-half as well as in his usual striking role. One of the best headers in the Premiership and proof that nice guys can succeed in the game.

Consistent Wales midfielder **MARK DELANEY** was hitting some of his best form when injury struck but he bounced back to show he had lost none of his skill after a prolonged abscence. Was one of the first players the Villa board tied down to a new contract as soon as they got a chance.

HEROES FUTURE

JLLOYD SAMUEL looks like he will play a left-sided defensive role, but the England Under-21 star is willing to take up any position if it means a game. In fact, he's played most positions across the back and in midfield, and handled all of the jobs to his boss's satisfaction. A player who is learning his trade at every opportunity.

Striker **STEFAN MOORE** made a big impression when he got into the Villa Park side and attracted the attenions of a number of other Premiership clubs. With The Villans since 2000, and signed a new long-term deal to ward off potential bargain hunters.

ASTON VILLA HERO
GARETH BARRY

BORN: February 23, 1981.
HEIGHT: 6ft.
CLUBS: Brighton.
WHY DO THEY LIKE HIM?
Versatile and loyal midfielder who gives 100 per cent.

BIRMINGHAM HERO

CHRISTOPHE DUGARRY

BORN: March 24, 1972, Bordeaux, France.
HEIGHT: 6ft 2in.
CLUBS: St. Seurin Girondins, Bordeaux (twice), AC Milan, Barcelona, Marseille.
WHY DO THEY LIKE HIM? He helped them fight off relegation during their first year in the Premiership.

BIRMINGHAM CITY

THE LATCHFORD BROTHERS made an impression for Birmingham City at opposite ends of the pitch. Bob was a prolific striker and elder brother Dave a keeper who made 239 appearances.

Frank Worthington, Trevor Francis were two other hitmen who made a big name for themselves at St. Andrews, whilst central defender Steve Bruce (left) the current boss, earned cult status after joining them following his title-winning career at Man United.

Midfielder Howard Kendall, later to be a manager, spent three years with City after joining them as part of the deal that saw Bob Latchford move to Everton.

Bob Hatton, a record buy in 1971, hit 73 goals in 218 games for Birmingham in less than five years, which turned out to be his longest spell with any one club.

And way back in 1984, then boss Jim Smith forked out £100,000 to take goalkeeper David Seaman to the club from Peterborough. He helped them to promotion.

HEROES PAST

WHEN YOU start to talk about powerful strikers the name of **BOB LATCHFORD** (1968-74) has to be included. He scored twice in his debut in 1969 against Preston and just a few months later turned out for England Youth. He notched up 84 goals in 194 games.

TREVOR FRANCIS was another hero in a blue shirt. As a 16-year-old he was a boy wonder and became the country's first £1m player when bought by Nottingham Forest boss Brian Clough after nine years with City (1970-79). But his return to the club as their manager just couldn't live up to the same high standards the fans expected.

HEROES PRESENT

YOUNG PLAYER of the season in 1999-2000 **DARREN PURSE** put an end to speculation linking him to Arsenal when he signed a new deal after Steve Bruce's arrival. A commanding figure in defence, the former England Under-21 player has also been used as an emergency striker.

If he plays for you he's great, if he plays for the opposition you hate him. But you can't deny that fiery Wales midfielder **ROBBIE SAVAGE** will give you his all. A totally committed player who just wants to win. His temperament might be a bit suspect at times, but he is a 100 per cent man.

HEROES FUTURE

MOST PUNDITS were baffled when Arsenal allowed defender **MATTHEW UPSON** to join City following a successful loan spell with Reading. But The Gunners' loss was The Blues' gain. Matt has blossomed under boss Steve Bruce into an England international.

At the age of 18, **DARREN CARTER** was given one of the biggest tasks in Birmingham's history – scoring the penalty in the play-off final shoot-out against Norwich that took the West Midlanders to the Premiership. A locally-born midfielder who has come through the club's Academy, youth and reserve sides.

WILD ROVERS
BLACKBURN

THERE ARE QUITE a few players from Blackburn's fairly recent past who will go down in history, most notably for helping them to win the Premiership crown in season 1994-95.

The likes of Chris Sutton, Alan Shearer, Tim Sherwood, Tim Flowers and David Batty all moved on to pastures new having helped Kenny Dalglish's side to the big prize.

But thanks for their success, and their current status as a team that should always be given respect, should perhaps go to one man: the late Jack Walker. The chairman ploughed millions of his own cash into the team he loved so much, so that they could become a major force.

Even though he has gone, a trust ensures that Blackburn will be able to compete and it helped them lure players of the calibre of Andy Cole and Dwight Yorke to add to home grown stars such as Republic of Ireland winger Damien Duff, and England midfielder David Dunn.

Above: Chris Sutton had an important role in the title victory.
Left: Rovers won the Worthington Cup under Souness

HEROES PAST

HE MIGHT NOT have been the most gifted footballer in the world, but **SIMON GARNER** (1978-92) will go down in Blackburn folklore. He was slow but skilfull and is the club's record goalscorer with 168. The Ewood fans still call his name.

They often boo him now, but **ALAN SHEARER's** goals were vital when Rovers grabbed the Premiership crown and the true fans know just how important Big Al was to their side (1992-96) before his record £15m move to Newcastle. With Chris Sutton he formed the striking partnership known as the SAS (based on their surnames) that proved so deadly.

HEROES PRESENT

NOW CLUB CAPTAIN, midfielder **GARY FLITCROFT** joined Rovers' from Manchester City in March 1996 for £3.2m. The player born just down the road in the land of rivals Bolton, has battled back from a number of injuries

USA goalkeeper **BRAD FRIEDEL** has emerged as one of the country's best men between the sticks since his arrival at Ewood Park from Liverpool in 2000. Boss Graeme Souness knew him from his Anfield days and his faith in the big man has been totally justified. A key to Rovers staying up during their first year back in the Premiership.

HEROES FUTURE

YOUNG ENGLAND DEFENDER **JAMES McEVELEY** made his debut in season 2002-03 after impressing in the reserves. It's now time for him to stake a claim for a regular first-team spot.

CIARAN DONNELLY scored four times for England Under-19s against Romania in the last European Championships and turned on a performance that could bode very well for his future. He has also played for England Under-16s and was part of the FA's Platinum club which aims to encourage the best young prospects. Signed for the club on his 14th birthday.

BLACKBURN HERO

ANDY COLE

BORN: Nottingham, Oct 15, 1971
HEIGHT: 5ft 11in
CLUBS: Arsenal, Fulham (loan)
Bristol City, Newcastle,
Man United.
WHY DO THEY LIKE HIM?
Quite simple: give him the ball
and he will score a goal.

BOLTON HERO
JAY JAY OKOCHA

BORN: August 14, 1973, Nigeria.
HEIGHT: 5ft 8in.
CLUBS: Paris St. Germain, Rangers (Nigeria), Eintracht Frankfurt, Fenerbahce.
WHY DO THEY LIKE HIM? He's one of the most exciting and skillful ball players Bolton have ever had.

TOP TROTTERS

BOLTON

NAT LOFTHOUSE scored 30 goals in 32 internationals for England and hit a further 252 for Wanderers in the league before injury forced his retirement in 1960. He had joined their ground staff in 1939 and was 1953 Footballer of the Year.

He later joined the club's coaching staff and became manager before taking up a role as club president.

A 16-year-old amateur player called Francis Lee, later to make his name at Man City, made his debut for Bolton in 1960, alongside Lofthouse, who was then already 35.

In the 1920s, David Jack, was sold to Arsenal for a then record fee of £10,500. In 1966, a new record of £80,000 was set when Wales striker Wyn Davies left for Newcastle.

The 1960s also produced keeper Eddie Hopkinson who made a record 519 league appearances. The club's youth policy gave us current manager Sam Allardyce, Leeds boss Peter Reid. Scottish striker John McGinlay was a more recent signing in the 1990s.

Above: Per Frandsen led the Scandinavian invasion at The Reebok.
Right: Current boss Sam Allardyce came through the youth system at Bolton.

HEROES PAST

FRANK WORTHINGTON (1977-79) played 81 games and scored 35 times for Bolton after arriving from Leicester. He moved on to Birmingham, Leeds and a host of other sides. A player with a confident swagger and a playboy image who the fans loved.

GUDNI BERGSSON (1995-2003) arrived in England from Iceland with countryman Eidur Gudjohnsen, but joined Bolton for £115000 after seven years with Spurs. Despite at least three attempts to call it a day he played on until last season when he finally quit at the age of 37, and headed home to become a solicitor.

HEROES PRESENT

MOST FANS wouldn't believe that France World Cup-winner **YOURI DJORKAEFF** was willing to sign for Bolton. But he did, and has proved to be more than just a one season wonder. His finishing powers are superb, but his all-round play is also a joy to watch.

Although Finland keeper **JUSSI JAASKELAINEN** had one season at The Reebok where he lost form and his place in the side, he has since proved a bargain £100,000 buy from VPS Vassa (1997). An excellent shot-stopper he has worked with Bolton's coaches to improve is all-round game and make himself undisputed No.1

HEROES FUTURE

KEVIN NOLAN is a Liverpool lad who came through the Bolton Academy. At 6ft 1in he can play in defence, but is used more in a midfield role. He scored on his debut against Chelsea but often saves his best performances for those fierce clashes against local rivals Manchester United.

JONATHAN WALTERS is another Scouser coming through the ranks after he was signed for £30,000 from the Academy of neighbours Blackburn Rovers. Just 20, much is expected of this forward, although boss Sam Allardyce has warned he is going to ease him into the team slowly.

77

ACE ADDICKS
CHARLTON

TODAY THE ADDICKS might be regarded as a small club who do well on average crowds but The Valley used to be massive ground attracting up to 75,000 fans to their games.

Sam Bartram was their greatest keeper and player after 579 league games between 1934 and 1956. He was also their oldest league player, turning out at 42.

At the other end of the pitch Eddie Firmani made 177 appearances and scored 89 goals before moving to Sampdoria for a then-record £35,000 in 1955. After also playing for Inter and Genoa he managed Charlton.

Midfielder Robert Lee was sold to Newcastle to save the club from going out of business after making 298 appearances for them and scoring 65 goals. He is still given a hero's welcome. Don't forget 1977 European Footballer of the Year Allan Simonsen and Danny Mills who went to Leeds in a record £4.3m deal in 1999.

Above: Chris Powell won a call up to the England squad in his 30s.
Left: Clive Mendonca was a prolific scorer for Athletic.

HEROES PAST

STRIKER **DEREK HALES** (1973-85) known as "Killer" for his lethal finishing in the penalty area, still has cult status at Charlton for his club record 168 goals in 320 appearances. Later moved to Gillingham. Their former manager Keith Peacock played 533 times for Athletic before returning in a as coaching role.

MIKE FLANAGAN (1971-86) was often a more than capable partner for Hales and during his 347 games for the club hit 120 goals. Incredibly, both he and Hales were sent off for fighting each other in an FA Cup tie against Maidstone! Later coached Charlton.

HEROES PRESENT

AFTER SPELLS with Coventry, Ipswich and York, keeper **DEAN KIELY** moved to The Valley in 1999 from Bury for £1m. Has just quit the Republic of Ireland squad, where he was No.2 choice, to concentrate on club football. Was Player of the Year in 2002.

SCOTT PARKER, born just down the road in Lambeth, is one of The Valley's own, having come through their youth system. The midfielder has already played for England Schools, Youth and Under-21s and is on the verge of being a regular for the senior side. Not bad for someone who used to work in a McDonalds, cleaning up the mess!

HEROES FUTURE

DEFENDER **JON FORTUNE** had a couple of spells on loan at Mansfield Town and that did the former Athletic trainee no harm at all and he is now a first-team squad regular who looks at ease in the Premiership. Born just over the River Thames in Islington.

MICHAEL TURNER is a central defender who spent some time in Italy as part of Charlton's link up with Serie A giants Inter, and has played in all of Athletic's junior sides, right up to the reserves. A good reader of the game, with good heading ability, he is expected to break into the first-team set-up very soon.

CHARLTON HERO

JASON EUELL

BORN: February 5, 1977, Lambeth, South London.
HEIGHT: 6ft.
CLUBS: Wimbledon.
WHY DO THEY LIKE HIM? He was their record buy and can play in a number of positions.

TRUE BLUES

CHELSEA

Above: Cup Winners Cup victory for The Blues, Zola and Vialli.
Right: Who could doubt Dennis Wise's dedication to the Chelsea cause?

LEGENDS AND STAMFORD BRIDGE appear to go hand-in-hand. From the days when hardman Ron Harris formed a brick wall in their defence to the current era when Franco Zola runs rings around the opposition, life at Chelsea has always been interesting. Throw in a few tantrums and a bit of solid determination from Dennis Wise and some deadly striking from Jimmy Floyd Hasselbaink and there is nearly always something for King's Road regulars to savour. Do you remember the giant central defender Micky Droy or the headed goals of Kerry Dixon?

Graeme Le Saux, in his second spell at The Bridge after a time with Blackburn Rovers, takes his place in history not just for his displays, but also as one of only two Channel Islanders – along with Matt le Tissier – to play in the Premiership.

France legends Didier Deschamps and Marcel Desailly were two players to take part in the multi-national revolution in West London, started by former player and boss Gianluca Vialli.

HEROES PAST

IN THE DAYS when defenders could do their jobs and referees didn't blow their whistles for the slightest of touches on players, **RON 'CHOPPER' HARRIS** (1961-1980) was still rated as one of the hardest men around. His job was to break up attacks and he did just that with total efficiency.

PETER OSGOOD (1964-74 and 1978-1980) was a striker of great ability – a real terrace hero. Even when he left to spend a few years with Southampton, he wasn't forgotten. Now he spends time at the ground handling corporate events, when allowed by chairman Ken Bates, himself a legend!

HEROES PRESENT

CARLO CUDICINI was an unknown keeper when he arrived at Stamford Bridge in 1999 for just £160,000. But he has gone on to prove himself one of the best around. Has been in England long enough to qualify for this country, but still fancies his chances of a place in the Italian national side.

Former boss Gianluca Vialli bought his friend **GIANFRANCO ZOLA** in 1996 and he has proved one of the best, if not *the* best, imports into English football. Fast, skilled, with a great eye for a goal and a pass he can turn a game in minutes. Nearer 40 than 30 he is still one of the fittest player around.

HEROES FUTURE

BERLIN-BORN defender **ROBERT HUTH** isn't 20 until August 2004 but his ball-winning skills for Chelsea's reserve side are already legendary. Amazingly, The Blues got him for free from Union Berlin.

CARLTON COLE signed for Chelsea as a teenager in 2000 and his goalscoring exploits since breaking into the first-team have earned him a five-year contract, something virtually unheard of these days. Already in the England Under-21 squad, he has pace, a quick turn for a tall striker and is already being hailed as one of the new big stars of King's Road. A finisher who shoots on sight.

TASTY TOFFEES
EVERTON

EVERTON may have had a few years in the doldrums until the arrival of boss David Moyes, but you could nearly always rely on them to produce a few memorable players.

How about: battling midfielder Peter Reid, leaping striker Joe Royle (yes, that's right, the current Ipswich boss) and even the free-scoring Gary Lineker, now of BBC Match of the Day fame, and top Sky Sports pundit Andy Gray who also got among the Goodison goals? Some tasty names there!

The legendary Peter Beardsley even had a spell in a blue shirt following his successful days across Stanley Park at big rivals Liverpool, and sandwiched between his two spells with home-town club Newcastle United.

Graham Sharpe was a legendary Scottish striker with The Toffees long before fellow countryman Duncan Ferguson had the club's name tattooed on his body. Sharpey still works for the Merseysiders.

Above: Yes, it's him, Sky Sports' Andy Gray.
Left: Wales keeper Neville Southall was a great servant to Everton.

HEROES PAST

FOR POWER, SKILL and sheer determination you wouldn't look much further than the 6ft 4in frame of Scotland striker **DUNCAN FERGUSON**. Fantastic in the air, the pigeon fancier (yes, they are his hobby) first joined Everton in 1994, helped them to the FA Cup the following season, then had two injury-hit years at Newcastle, before returning in 2000 to a hero's welcome.

Now Leeds boss, **PETER REID** joined Everton for £600,000 in 1982 and stayed for seven years, the last two acting as player-coach to another legend in these parts, Colin Harvey.

HEROES PRESENT

THE ARRIVAL OF striker **KEVIN CAMPBELL** in 1999 from Turkish side Trabzonspor was an immediate success for the former Arsenal player with nine goals in just eight games. Appointed club captain in 2001, the first black player to be given the armband.

DAVID WEIR, like Campbell signed by former boss Walter Smith in 1999, cost just a nominal fee from Hearts but has proved to be consistent at the heart of the defence, also skippering the side at one stage. Gave up his Scotland career so he could concentrate on his club career, and a definite favourite on the terraces.

HEROES FUTURE

INJURIES HAVE HELD back the development of defender **TONY HIBBERT**, who is rated as one of the best tacklers at the club, over the past season or so. Already part of the junior England ranks, the Merseysider was a part of the club's FA Youth Cup-winning side of 1998, which also included Wayne Rooney.

Defender **SEAN O'HANLON** is hoping that he can follow team-mate Rooney through the England Under-20 system in his bid for stardom. Just 20 in 2003, Sean is set for a breakthrough and has the right manager to guide him in David Moyes.

EVERTON HERO
WAYNE ROONEY

BORN: Liverpool, Oct 24, 1985.
HEIGHT: 5ft 10in
CLUBS: Everton from trainee.
WHY DO THEY LIKE HIM?
Come on! This is Roonaldo, one of their own and England's big hope.

LOUIS SAHA

BORN: August 8, 1978, Paris, France.
HEIGHT: 5ft 9in.
CLUBS: Metz, Newcastle (loan).
WHY DO THEY LIKE HIM?
He's an exciting but entirely
unpredictable goalscorer.

COTTAGE KINGS
FULHAM

Above: Scottish midfielder John Collins was brought back to Britain by Jean Tigana. **Right:** Mullery and Moore, great players for Fulham.

IT MIGHT BE hard to believe, but the great George Best once played for Fulham. They have also included England's World Cup-winning skipper Bobby Moore among their ranks and even current Newcastle boss Sir Bobby Robson turned out at The Cottage.

Kevin Keegan will probably be one of their best remembered managers, but who would have thought they could tempt former France star Jean Tigana into the gaffer's chair?

Or that they would fork out a sack full of cash to land top Holland goalkeeper Edwin van der Saar?

But before those heady days with chairman Mohamed Al Fayed millions, remember there were players such as England skipper Johnny Haynes (1952-1970); George Cohen, Alan Mullery (now a TV pundit); Malcolm Macdonald; Micky Adams who guided them to promotions; strikers Viv Busby and John Mitchell. And there has to be a mention for former chairman Jimmy Hill, who saved the club from extinction.

HEROES PAST

DO WE REALLY have to say anything much about the skills of Irishman **GEORGE BEST**? He played 48 times for Fulham and scored eight goals (1976-78). During the summer break he played for Los Angeles Aztecs.

Wales striker **GORDON DAVIES** (1978-91) is still Fulham's record league goalscorer with 159 to his credit, 180 in total. He also won 16 caps for Wales between 1979-86, 14 of them whilst he was at Fulham, the other two after a move to Manchester City, and scored twice. He is also their leading scorer in the top flight with 24 in the old Division One in 1982.

HEROES PRESENT

BORN JUST DOWN the road in Clapham **SEAN DAVIS** has always been highly rated by his managers at Fulham and has played for them through every division up to the Premiership. An England Under-21 star who could break into the senior set-up if he can find some consistency in midfield where he is a no-nonsense performer.

SYLVAIN LEGWINSKI was a player who followed boss Tigana to The Cottage from Monaco, just like John Collins. He cost them just over £3m at the start of season 2001-02 and dominates the centre of midfield, as well as being able to grab the occasional vital goal.

HEROES FUTURE

TO CALL **ZAT (ZATYIAH) KNIGHT** a big prospect for Fulham would be an understatement. He may not have the biggest frame, but at 6ft 6in he's certainly one of the tallest defenders around. Has played for England Under-21 and with a bit more experience should get a few more regular games for his club. Also plays midfield.

Last season proved a break-through one for Ghana-born striker **ELVIS HAMMOND** and he showed enough promise to earn himself a new contract. His close ball control and quick bursts of speed are his strong points. Had a season-long loan at Bristol Rovers.

YORKSHIRE TERRIERS
LEEDS

BACK IN THE 1960S-70s the Leeds United team built up under manager Don Revie won trophies galore and turned all of their players into household names.

Led by Scotsman Billy Bremner, it included people like striker Allan Clarke, hardman Norman Hunter, defender Paul Reaney and Peter Lorimer, the man with the hardest shot in football at the time.

To give you a clue as to just how famous they were, just imagine the Manchester United team of today and their world-renown stars like Beckham, van Nistelrooy, Giggs and Keane.

The past couple of years may not have been the best in United's history but in previous decades they really were a force to be reckoned. Remember they also had people like now-Southampton boss Gordon Strachan, Frenchman Eric Cantona (before he went to Manchester United) and the silky skills of Gary McAllister.

Above: Don Revie, back far left, and his 1970s side.
Below: David Batty has had two spells at Leeds.

HEROES PAST

AFTER HIS EARLY career at Aberdeen **GORDON STRACHAN** joined former boss Alex Ferguson at Manchester United before what appeared to be a downward move to Leeds. How wrong can you be? The flame-haired Scotsman showed no dip in his form as he battled his way through the Leeds midfield (1989-95).

Years before Strach, it was another hot-headed Scot, **BILLY BREMNER,** who really put the bite into the Leeds United midfield (1959-76). So great was his influence on the side they erected a statue of the player outside of the Elland Road in his honour.

HEROES PRESENT

REPUBLIC OF IRELAND defender **IAN HARTE** will be forever remembered for some of his glorious, hammer-hard free-kicks. A quiet man off the pitch he has stamped his authority at either full-back or in midfield.

Signed from Charlton for £4m in 1999 full-back **DANNY MILLS** played his way into England's 2002 World Cup Finals squad. His biggest problem was his temper that made fans worry about how many cards he would pick up. But in the Far East Danny kept his cool, showed great spirit and fully deserved the confidence placed in him by boss Sven Goran Eriksson.

HEROES FUTURE

THE SEASON 2002-03 will be remembered for a number of bad reasons by Leeds fans, but they will also celebrate the arrival of teenage winger **JAMES MILNER** who became the Premiership's youngest goalscorer in December 2002 when he was still a month away from his 17th birthday.

Goalkeeper **SHAUN ALLAWAY** was signed in the summer of 2000 from Reading despite interest by Spurs. His early Elland Road career held back by a wrist injury, but with guidance from both Nigel Martyn and Paul Robinson is destined to become one of his country's finest between the posts.

LEEDS HERO

ALAN SMITH

BORN: October 28, 1980, Leeds.
HEIGHT: 5ft 9in.
CLUBS: Leeds from trainee.
WHY DO THEY LOVE HIM? He's a local lad who just wants to see United win and gives it his all.

LEICESTER HERO
MUZZY IZZET

BORN: October 31, 1979, Mile End, East London.
HEIGHT: 5ft 10in.
CLUBS: Chelsea.
WHY DO THEY LIKE HIM? Stuck with Leicester even when they were relegated from the Premiership.

FAVE FOXES
LEICESTER

ONE OF ENGLAND'S greatest-ever keepers began his route to the top with Leicester City, World Cup-winning Gordon Banks.

He arrived at Filbert Street from Chesterfield in 1959 for £6,000 and was a losing finalist in two FA Cup Finals in 1961 and 1963, before Leicester beat Stoke City in the 1964 League Cup Final.

Banksy let in just three goals in the 1966 World Cup Finals, and then moved to Stoke for £52,000 the following season.

Incredibly, his No.1 shirt was taken over by another future England keeper, Peter Shilton, who kept an amazing 23 clean sheets as Leicester won the Division Two title in 1970-71. Shilts later made the same move as Banks to Stoke City.

Londoner Alan Birchenall arrived at the club as a striker after turning out for many sides, including Chelsea, but it was in midfield where he showed his best form under legendary manager Jimmy Bloomfield. Steve Walsh scored two goals in the 1993-94 Division One play off final to beat Derby.

Above: Emile Heskey left Leicester for Liverpool in an £11m deal. **Right:** Boss Martin O'Neill and defender Matt Elliott were two big influences for The Foxes.

HEROES PAST

GARY LINEKER (1976-85) is probably Leicester's most famous son in recent times. Born in the city, he even led the consortium that saved the club from extinction last season. Played 194 games and scored 95 goals before moving to Everton, Barcelona and Spurs. His 48 England goals make him second only to Bobby Charlton.

ALAN SMITH (1982-87) scored 84 goals for the club in 206 games before a £850,000 move to Arsenal. Also won 13 England caps. Was Lineker's substitute in the national side when Gary was pulled off early, preventing him for scoring a record number of goals.

HEROES PRESENT

MATT ELLIOTT had already been a journeyman player with Charlton, Torquay and Scunthorpe before a £1.6m move to The Foxes in 1997 from Oxford. His performances at the centre of the defence earned him a call up from Scotland. His finest moment was as Man of the Match at Wembley in 2000, when he scored two against Tranmere to win the Worthington Cup 2-1.

IAN WALKER arrived at Leicester from Spurs for £2.5m after struggling to hold on to his place at White Hart Lane where he was even loaned out to Oxford. Has since recaptured his form and earned an England recall.

HEROES FUTURE

STRIKER **TOMMY WRIGHT** scored so many goals for City's Academy that he earned a call up to the senior squad. Still a teenager, he took the England Under-19 place of Wayne Rooney and has been likened to a young Gary Lineker, who profiled the youngster during a recent BBC programme. Tommy's family have been ticket holders since Gary's days at the club.

Unlucky **JORDAN STEWART** has two dislocated shoulders to blame for holding back his career. But following a loan spell with Bristol Rovers in 2000, he has proven useful in both the left-back and left midfield positions.

ANFIELD ACES
LIVERPOOL

DURING THE 1970S and for some of the 1980s Liverpool were THE team that everyone wanted to beat and their sides were full of players who could be named in every household.

Staunton, Dalglish, Keegan, Lawrenson, Hansen, Grobbelaar, Kennedy - yes, Anfield could be a very lonely place during those weeks when there were international games taking place.

Even the managers made rival teams quake with fear - Bill Shankly, Joe Fagan plus Bob Paisley who won more than them all! Now it's Gerard Houllier who helped them to the Worthington, UEFA and FA Cups in 2001!

But the likes of England skipper Emlyn Hughes, tough tackling defender (and we mean TOUGH) Tommy Smith, deadly strikers John Toshack and John Aldridge plus tricky winger John Barnes and midfield dynamo Peter Beardsley have all earned their places in the Anfield archives.

Above: Gerard Houllier got Liverpool among the trophies. **Left:** Alan Hansen, now a BBC pundit.

HEROES PAST

KENNY DALGLISH might not have been the boss fans expected when he took over the manager's chair, but as a player he was their idol. A skillful and creative striker. A player from 1977 to 1990 after a £440,000 move from Celtic and manager from 1985-1991.

Record goal scorer **IAN RUSH** will forever be the man they talk about as the legendary centre-forward. The Wales star's reputation earned him a £3.2m move to Juventus in 1987 but after just one season he was back on Merseyside and again banging in the goals. Scored 346 goals in 658 appearances for The Reds.

HEROES PRESENT

MICHAEL OWEN has been knocking in goals for so long that you tend to forget that he is still only 25 in 2004. Has already equalled Rushy's European scoring record for The Reds. Made his debut at the age of 17, after coming through the ranks and is destined to become England's top scorer and appearance maker.

Skipper SAMI **HYYPIA** arrived at Liverpool for £2.6m in the summer of 1999 and has since carved out a reputation as a strong, reliable central defender who can also move up field to score vital goals. A massive favourite among the Kop regulars, a Mr. Reliable.

HEROES FUTURE

THE arrival of a whole host of foreign players hasn't dampened the chances of youngsters coming through the ranks at Anfield. Striker **NEIL MELLOR,** whose dad Ian played for Manchester City, is a tall, strong, typical old fashioned centre-forward who made his first-team debut late in 2002.

JOHN WELSH is a midfielder who has been likened to Steve Gerrard and as a Liverpool-born teenager he could be destined for superstardom with his local club. He's been with the club since he was just ten-years-old and it won't be long before he is representing his country at junior levels.

MANCHESTER CITY HERO
ALI BENARBIA

BORN: August 10, 1968, Algeria.
HEIGHT: 5ft 7in.
CLUBS: Paris St. Germain, Bordeaux.
WHY DO THEY LIKE HIM?
He's exciting, committed and can
turn a game in an instant.

MAINE MEN
MAN CITY

Above:
Shaun Goater was a deadly striker for Man City.

Right:
Georgian Georgi Kinkladze at Maine Road.

IN RECENT YEARS the blue half of Manchester has had to live in the shadow of their all-conquering neighbours United, but over the years City have had their fair share of stars.

Legendary Scotland hitman Denis Law played for both sides but his goal that will live on forever was the only one in the derby game of 1974, an effort which sent United down to the old Second Division for the first time in 36 years.

Rodney Marsh had four years at Maine Road after leaving QPR; big Niall Quinn had six years with City and etched himself into history with four goals during derby matches with United.

Dennis Tueart, now a director, joined City from Sunderland and scored their winning goal in a 2-1 defeat of Newcastle United in the League Cup Final.

Winger Mike Summerbee played at the club during the 1960s and 70s and was followed by son Nicky in the 90s. Don't forget his team-mate Tony Book with 291 appearances.

HEROES PAST

HE LOOKED TOO tubby to be a top goalscorer, but **FRANCIS LEE** (1967-74) was deadly when he got the ball anywhere near the area. He was also their penalty taking king and hit a remarkable ten goals during derby games with Manchester United. Later returned to the club as chairman.

COLIN BELL (1966-79) scored eight derby game goals against United, quite a tally for a player regarded as a midfielder. He was nicknamed "Nijinsky" by his team-mates after a famous racehorse of the day. Bought from Bury for £45,000 he went on to collect 48 England caps.

HEROES PRESENT

ROBBIE FOWLER was a massive hit at Liverpool but after a big money move never really settled at Leeds United. Often referred to as one of England's best natural finishers, Robbie appears to be finally finding his feet at Maine Road – and that can only be bad news for opposing defenders!

Everyone expected French striker **NIC ANELKA** to sign for Liverpool after a successful loan spell, but the former Arsenal man was lured to Manchester by Kevin Keegan. A natural goal-scorer, Nic has courted controversy, although no one should doubt his ability to turn defences inside out.

HEROES FUTURE

WHEN YOUR DAD was a noted player, it's always going to be difficult to make a name of your own, but **SHAUN WRIGHT-PHILLIPS** hasn't let that stand in his way. Son of former Arsenal goal ace Ian Wright, Shaun has also knocked for six the idea that if you aren't that tall you can't be a pro. Has earnt himself a place with the England Under-21 squad.

JOE BARTON hails from Liverpool and has been likened to his big mate Steve Gerrard and his boss Kevin Keegan. But Joe is his own man and reckons he plays more of a roaming role in midfield. Great worker who could go far.

SIMPLY REDS
MAN UNITED

NO MATTER WHAT age you are some of the greatest players ever to pull on the red shirt of Manchester United will be stamped on your brain - probably starting with George Best.

From that same era the names of Denis Law and Bobby Charlton will also spring to mind followed by great stars such as Denmark goalkeeper Peter Schmeichel and the amazing, match-winning skills of sometimes wayward French striker Eric Cantona.

Sir Alex Ferguson will go down as their greatest-ever manager for his incredible haul of silverware at Old Trafford, despite following in the footsteps of Sir Matt Busby who had two great spells at the club.

The youngsters who all burst through into the first-team together - Beckham, the Nevilles, Butt, Scholes, Giggs and friends - will rightly reserve a place in history, but don't forget the likes of Steve Bruce and Bryan Robson earlier.

Above: Champs of Europe in 1999 under Fergie.
Left: Roy Keane has been United's inspirational skipper

HEROES PAST

HE WAS HAILED as one of the greatest players ever, football's first playboy megastar and **GEORGE BEST** (1962-73) lived up to his billing. The Northern Ireland forward was the David Beckham of his day, except he had more than just one gorgeous girl on his arm and would be spotted with more than one drink in his hand!

ERIC CANTONA (1992-97) was the striker they couldn't control in France and after just one season at Leeds he moved to bitter rivals United for just £1m. A bargain! It was worth paying the ticket money to watch his skills. For The Red Devils his signing meant cups!

HEROES PRESENT

FORGET THE CLOTHES, strange hair styles and jet-set life - **DAVID BECKHAM** has the style to get away with all of that and still parade his skills on the pitch. A good player, he showed his greatness after taking on the England armband. Will be sadly missed by many at Old Trafford.

RUUD VAN NISTELROOY suffered a horrific knee injury that delayed his £19m move from PSV Eindhoven to Old Trafford. But the sack full of goals he has scored since his arrival proved it was worth the wait. He might look a bit awkward on the pitch but his skill and deadly shooting are awesome.

HEROES FUTURE

YOU MAY HAVE heard lots of players referred to as the new Ryan Giggs, but **KIERAN RICHARDSON** could just be the midfielder to live up to that description. He's battled his way through the Academy after signing from West Ham and earned his first-team squad place just over a year ago at the age of 17. Another player with a massive challenge is **DARREN FLETCHER** - the next David Beckham! Just 20 in 2004, he's already 6ft tall and Scotland are keeping a close eye on the youngster who was chased hard by Sir Alex Ferguson who didn't want to miss out on him.

RIO FERDINAND

BORN: Peckham, November 8, 1978.
HEIGHT: 6ft 2in.
CLUBS: West Ham, Bournemouth (loan), Leeds United.
WHY DO THEY LIKE HIM?
Strong, good on the ball and still learning.

MIDDLESBROUGH HERO
JUNINHO

BORN: February 22, 1973 Sao Paulo.
HEIGHT: 1.67m
CLUBS: Flamengo, Vasco da Gama, Atletico Madrid.
WHY DO THEY LIKE HIM? He has superb skills and is a match-winner

BORO'S BEST

MIDDLESBROUGH

THE WORLD WAS stunned when a 5 ft 4in midfielder signed for The Boro for a then quite hefty £4.75m fee in 1995. It wasn't his height that caused the fans' eyebrows to be raised, it was the fact that Brazil's No.10 was on his way to Teesside. Juninho was his name and it was to be the start of his two spells with the club. There had been many big name players in the past, ranging from Wilf Mannion, John Hickton and even England's first £500,000 player, David Mills, but this buy by boss Bryan Robson was a masterstroke.

The hard battling boy from Brazil proved to be an amazing player who quickly won over the terraces. Club finances after relegation meant he was off-loaded to Atletico Madrid, but he was later loaned back before Middlesbrough eventually ensured his return to The Riverside on a permanent basis in season 2002-03. The return of the prodigal son.

Above: Bryan Robson celebrates the capture of Juninho.
Left: Local lad David Mills left Boro for £500,000.

HEROES PAST

SCOTTISH STRIKER **BERNIE SLAVEN** hit 146 goals in 381 games for Boro during 1985-93 and was a firm favourite during the days at Ayresome Park.

He still covers the club's matches for local radio in the North East and they haven't really replaced him with a quality striker who can get 20 goals a season.

GARY PALLISTER made his name at Middlesbrough between 1984-89 before his qualities got him a £2.5m move to Manchester United where he helped them to bags of silverware with defensive partner Steve Bruce. Returned to Boro for 1998-2000.

HEROES PRESENT

GARETH SOUTHGATE may have joined Boro late in his career, but the England defender, converted from a midfielder during his time at Aston Villa, soon showed what a cultured play he is on the pitch. He also adds leadership qualities to a side and when things are going wrong Gareth is the man to turn to for inspiration.

JONATHAN GREENING didn't quite make the grade at Man United, but boss Steve McClaren went back to his old club after taking over the manager's job at Boro and signed the midfielder for £2m. Won two player of the year awards in 2002-03.

HEROES FUTURE

AUSTRALIAN DEFENDER **LUKE WILKSHIRE** signed for Middlesbrough as a professional in 2001 when boss Bryan Robson was still in charge at The Riverside. He made his debut in March 2002 against Southampton and since then his number of appearances for the first-team have been on the increase, as well as his reputation with his team-mates.

Durham-born **STUART PARNABY** has already appeared for England Under-21s and is a full-back who loves to get forward. As a local lad he will be looked on favourably, especially if he can maintain his development.

MIGHTY MAGPIES
NEWCASTLE

THERE HAVE BEEN some amazing players at Newcastle over the years but it is always the wearer of the famous No.9 shirt with black and white stripes that gets the most attention.

There's a monument of Jackie Milburn just outside of the ground; Malcolm Macdonald can still be seen at games; Andy Cole made his mark; but Alan Shearer is destined to become the shirt's most famous occupant.

He arrived at his home town club after a £15m move from Blackburn Rovers, a world record at the time, and part of the agreement was that he had the No.9, at that time worn by Les Ferdinand. Sir Les reluctantly handed over the number but failed to get No.99 which he wanted!

Kevin Keegan played his part in Geordie folklore both as a player and manager and Bobby Moncur is the skipper who helped The Magpies to the Inter Cities Fairs Cup, the forerunner of the EUFA Cup, back in 1969.

Above: Les Ferdinand was nicknamed Sir Les and still gets respect.
Left: Alan Shearer returns home for £15m.

HEROES PAST

MALCOLM McDONALD hit 95 goals in 187 games for Newcastle during 1971-77 to earn the nickname Supermac. A determined and out-and-out striker, he had no fear and would shoot on strike. Once scored five goals for England against Cyprus, still a record. Moved to Arsenal for £333,333.

A lot of modern day fans will tell you that **PETER BEARDSLEY** is the finest player ever to wear a Newcastle shirt during his two spells with the club 1983-87 and 1993-97. Although he played just behind the front two, Peter was a striker who did more than his fair share in midfield.

HEROES PRESENT

A LOT OF FANS questioned Ruud Gullit's decision to pay out £6m to Ipswich for midfielder **KIERON DYER**. The fans may not be happy about the way the Dutchman managed their side, but they now admit it was money well spent on a player with speed and skill.

SHAY GIVEN could have found life hard at St. James' Park as, earlier in his career, he was on loan at bitter local rivals Sunderland. But the Republic of Ireland's No.1 goalkeeper has proved to among the Premiership's best. He may not be the tallest keeper around, but Shay has proved an outstanding player.

HEROES FUTURE

JERMAINE JENAS is destined to become one of the greatest footballers of the next few years, according to all of those in the know, including England Under-21 boss David Platt. JJ has speed, bags of ability and knows no fear. He may only be 21 in 2004, but he has already shown that he can play with and against the best.

RICHARD OFFIONG is a teenage striker who Sir Bobby Robson loaned out to Darlington and Hearts in an attempt to give him experience. If the youngster can reward his boss's faith by taking the chance he has been offered, a bright future beckons.

NEWCASTLE HERO

ALAN SHEARER

BORN: August 13, Newcastle
HEIGHT: 6ft
OTHER CLUBS: Southampton, Blackburn Rovers.
WHY DO THEY LIKE HIM? He's a Geordie who gives his all for his home town club.

PORTSMOUTH HERO

PAUL MERSON

BORN: March 20, 1968, Harlesden, North West London.
HEIGHT: 6ft.
CLUBS: Brentford, Arsenal, Middlesbrough, Aston Villa.
WHY DO THEY LIKE HIM?
He dropped out of the Premiership to join them, and helped them to promotion.

POMPEY'S PRIDE
PORTSMOUTH

POMPEY are riding high after promotion to the Premiership for the first time, but for the past few decades there hasn't been a lot to shout about at Fratton Park.

You have to go back to season 1964-65 to find one of their most memorable occasions. That was when 20,000 fans crammed into the ground to say goodbye to Jimmy Dickinson who played a staggering 764 league games for the side and helped them to two league titles.

Some ten season later, under the guidance of former Liverpool star Ian St. John, Pompey crashed down to the old Third Division. Fast forward to 1987 when Alan Ball, the former England star, guided them back to Division One for the first time in 28 years, after they were runners-up.

The 1990s saw the emergence of Darren Anderton before he went to Spurs and in 2002 they collected a club record £5m fee for the sale of giant striker Peter Crouch to Villa.

Above: Harry Redknapp guided Pompey into the Premiership
Right: Darren Anderton turning on the skill that earned him a move to Tottenham.

HEROES PAST

GOALKEEPER **ALAN KNIGHT** received an MBE in 2000, for his services to football. Actually known as "The Legend", he made his debut for the side at the age of 16 in 1978 and turned out in an amazing 683 games before calling it a day in season 1999-2000 to help coach at Pompey, his only club.

Portsmouth-born striker **STEVE CLARIDGE** (1998-01) with his socks rolled down to his ankles may not have looked a threat, but everywhere he's played he's knocked in goals and been a fans' favourite. Loved here as he is regarded as the ultimate anti-Southampton follower!

HEROES PRESENT

ALTHOUGH BULGARIAN STRIKER **SVETOSLAV TODOROV** had shown glimpses of his true form at West Ham, it wasn't until he rejoined his former boss Harry Redknapp at Portsmouth that he proved his worth. Scored 26 league goals as Pompey got promoted and is rated by the gaffer as one of his shrewder signings.

Goalkeeper **SHAKA HISLOP** arrived on the South Coast via Reading, Newcastle and West Ham and his experience between the sticks proved invaluable. The Trinidad and Tobago international kept £1.8m then-record buy Yoshikatsu Kawaguchi sidelined.

HEROES FUTURE

DEFENDER **MATT TAYLOR** was on the shopping lists of quite a few clubs before Redknapp took the plunge and paid £400,000 to Luton for the youngster. His raiding play down the left wing and his much-improved performances during the season will have raised his value considerably.

GARRY O'NEILL is a home-grown midfielder, but it is his role on the opposite wing to Taylor that has earmarked the player as one to watch. Just 21, his first venture into the Premiership will give him the stage to show his true skills against the world's biggest stars. Both players have England hopes.

SUPER SAINTS
SOUTHAMPTON

THEY MAY NOT be the most fashionable side around but that hasn't stopped Southampton attracting some amazing players.

Kevin Keegan (right) Alan Shearer, Matt Le Tissier, Kevin Keegan, Peter Osgood and Alan Ball have all been Saints.

But the biggest Saint of all has to be Terry Paine who played a mind-numbing 801 times for Southampton and scored 183 goals. His only other club was Hereford for a further 106 games.

Winger Paine started his career just down the road with local side, Winchester, and signed on at The Dell in August 1956 and stayed there until 1974. During that time he earned 19 England caps, all of them as a Second Division player. He scored a hat-trick at Wembley against Czechoslovakia and awarded the MBE for services to football. Now lives in South Africa and does radio commentary.

Gordon Strachan promises to be one of their popular bosses to join the ranks of Ted Bates and "Big" Lawrie McMenemy. Then there was Bobby Stokes who scored the FA Cup-winning goal in 1976.

HEROES PAST

MICK CHANNON (1966-77) won 46 England caps and scored 21 goals for his country. One of the biggest memories of the man, now a successful racehorse trainer, was his windmill goal celebration. Played 718 league games and played for Man City, among others.

MATT LE TISSIER (1986-02) was often criticised for not taking his undoubted talents to another club. The critics said he was afraid of failing elsewhere. But the player known as "Le God", was happy at Saints and his totally loyalty to the side and his free-scoring ability from midfield means he will be forever etched in club history.

HEROES PRESENT

A FAVOURITE with the fans, **JO TESSEM** is a defender who has also been used in midfield and attack. Proved a dangerous addition to the side from the bench last season. He cost just £600,000 from Norway side Molde where the 6ft 3in star played in the Champions League.

Born in Southampton, **WAYNE BRIDGE** is a favourite with many England fans to take over the left-back spot where he thrives best in going forward. Until last season he had played more than two terms without missing a game, before injury struck. Has been the subject of much interest from big sides.

HEROES FUTURE

ENGLAND UNDER-21 midfielder **DAVID PRUTTON** had carved out quite a reputation for himself at Nottingham Forest before a move last year to St. Mary's. A strong ball-winner with an eye for a good pass, he has already started to win over Saints' fans.

Defender **CHRIS BAIRD** played all but five minutes of the FA Cup Final defeat to Arsenal and did enough that day to suggest he has a big future. He came from nowhere to earn his place and everyone expected him to get a roasting from The Gunners' star names. It never happened and he was Saints' star performer.

SOUTHAMPTON HERO
JAMES BEATTIE

BORN: February 27, 1978, Lancaster.
HEIGHT: 6ft 1in.
CLUBS: Blackburn.
WHY DO THEY LIKE HIM?
He's rode out criticism to show that he is a top goalscorer and earned a place in the England set-up.

TOTTENHAM HERO
ROBBIE KEANE

BORN: July 8, 1980, Dublin.
HEIGHT: 5ft 9in.
CLUBS: Wolves, Coventry, Inter Milan, Leeds.
WHY DO THEY LIKE HIM?
He's a classy goalscorer, full of running with bags of skill. Just what they like at White Hart Lane.

CRAFTY COCKERELS
TOTTENHAM

LIFE MAY NOT have been sweet at White Hart Lane in recent years, a trend not helped by a speedy revolving door for managers. But the club is historically noted for its classy football, dating back to when free-scoring Jimmy Greaves was part of their set-up.

They have loved their strikers, including Steve Archibald and Gary Lineker before they moved to Barcelona, and the legendary German Jurgen Klinsmann who had two stints at White Hart Lane, the second not quite as happy as the first, and the much-loved Les Ferdinand and Teddy Sheringham.

They've also had some pretty amazing midfielders, not least current boss Glenn Hoddle and Ossie Ardiles. The Argentinian had just collected the World Cup when he arrived in London, along with fellow countryman Ricky Villa who himself would go on and score a fantastic FA Cup-winning goal in 1981. And there was also the brilliant skills of French wing wizard David Ginola.

Above: Classy but inconsistent, French ace David Ginola.
Right: Gary Lineker with not a crisp in sight.

HEROES PAST

The arrival of **OSSIE ARDILES** (1978-88) in London was greeted with dropped jaws. But the same fans who could hardly believe the coup their club had pulled off were even more amazed when they saw his talents on the pitch. Shame his stint had to be interrupted by the Falklands War.

GLENN HODDLE(1975-87) played the game fans appreciated with creative midfield passing, even though he wasn't always valued at England level. His move to Monaco allowed his skills to develop further. Sadly, his management career hasn't always been as good as his playing one.

HEROES PRESENT

SIMON DAVIES arrived from Peterborough in a package with fellow midfielder Matt Etherington. Whilst Matt hasn't always been a regular, although he did get into the England Under-21s, Simon has blossomed into a fully fledged Wales international and been one of the first names on team sheets.

DEAN RICHARDS arrived at The Lane in an £8.1m move from Southampton, following boss Hoddle up the M3 shortly after he left the South Coast club. A player who dominates the back line in the air and on the deck and who is also always likely to cause damage in the opposition penalty area.

HEROES FUTURE

ANTHONY GARDNER is another lanky defender who will be looking to follow in Sol Campbell's boots. Even at 6ft 5in the England Under-21 player doesn't look cumbersome and has a lot of pace and skill for a man of his height.

STEPHEN KELLY had a great loan spell with QPR last season and even appeared for them in the Division Two play-off final. After coming through the ranks at White Hart Lane the extra experience he has picked up should stand him in good stead for the future. He finished the season with a call up to the Republic of Ireland Under-21 side who drew 2-2 with Germany.

GOLDEN BOYS
WOLVES

ROBBIE KEANE became the first Wolves player in more than 30 years to score a double on his debut when he hit two at Norwich on the opening day of the 1997-98 season. He hit two more in his fourth game and also became the Republic of Ireland's youngest-ever player.

Kenny Hibbitt had a much longer career in the famous gold shirt, playing for 16 years after joining them from Bradford Park Avenue in 1968. The midfielder helped them lift the League Cup in 1974 and 1980 and also ensured their promotion to the old First Division in both 1976-77 and 1982-83.

Wayne Clarke, brother of Leeds ace Allan, was with Wolves from 1977-84 and scored 33 goals in 170 games before moving to Birmingham. Further back in time, Billy Wright and Bill Slater both won the Football Writers' Footballer of the Year awards.

Above: Wolves take on Sheffield United in the play-off final. **Left:** Chairman Sir Jack Hayward and boss Dave Jones celebrate promotion.

HEROES PAST

STRIKER **STEVE BULL** will be regarded by many fans as Mr Wolves for his total dedication to the side (1986-99) despite their fall down the divisions. He stuck with them and scored the goals that helped them back up the leagues. He is their record league goalscorer with 246 goals and hit 300 in 544 games. Also scored on England debut.

Belfast-born **DEREK DOOGAN** joined Wolves in 1967 and during eight years scored 123 goals in 323 games and won 43 Northern Ireland caps. He returned to the club after his career finished as both chairman and chief executive.

HEROES PRESENT

SHAUN NEWTON got off to a great start, scoring on his Wolves debut at the start of the 2001-02 season after moving from Charlton for £850,000. The London-born player's hard work and willingness to track back and help the defence has made him a firm favourite with the Molineux crowd.

LEE NAYLOR has already played for England Youth and Under-21s, and if he can maintain good form, as a left-back he could find himself in demand for full England honours. Walsall-born, he was been with Wolves since signing as a trainee in 1997 and is already well past the 120 league appearances mark.

HEROES FUTURE

JOLEON LESCOTT grabbed his chance when he got into the side in 2001-02 and still only 21, he looks an outstanding prospect. Born in Birmingham, his brother Aaron plays for Stockport. Has played for England Under-21s.

MATT MURRAY has already taken over the England Under-21 goalkeeping shirt from Chris Kirkland and some of his brilliant saves in the Division One play-off final at Cardiff's Millennium Stadium will have opened a few more people's eyes. Made his debut at the start of last season after joining the club as a trainee in 1997 at the age of 16.

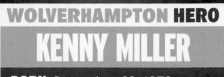

WOLVERHAMPTON HERO

KENNY MILLER

BORN: December 23, 1979,
Edinburgh.
HEIGHT: 5ft 9in.
CLUBS: Rangers, Hibs.
WHY IS HE LIKED? A gifted
goalscorer who has again found
his true form at Molineux.

SPILL THE BEANS!

IT'S GREAT WHEN FOOTBALL PEOPLE SAY WHAT THEY MEAN, EVEN IF THEY END UP SLIGHTLY RED-FACED!

'He's brilliant this boy, he knows more about football than me. Have you see what he's done? It's absolutely incredible."

Newcastle boss **SIR BOBBY ROBSON** could have been raving about the skills of a new signing, but he was actually ranting about the developer of a new computer game that he had put his name to.

"It frightens the life out of me when central defenders try and play football. Everyone raves about Rio Ferdinand but the first couple of times I watched him I had my heart in my mouth, he was constantly trying to control high balls and for me that is not what defending is about – get the thing clear!"

Former Republic boss and former England stopper **JACK CHARLTON** obviously favours no-nonsense players.

"My current room-mate is Alan Mahon (left) and he has this terrible habit of stinking the room out after a bowl or two of cereal. Before him I had the misfortune of sharing with Craig Hignett and he would ask if I would like a cup of tea and then disappear for three hours to play pool or go for a chat in one of the other lads' rooms. Charming!"

Blackburn's Aussie defender **LUCAS NEILL** reckons he should pick his friends more carefully.

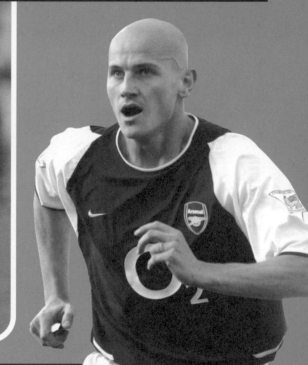

"I was also asking myself about (Pascal) Cygan and thinking: 'He's 28 years-old, where has he been? What has he done?' Of course, Arsene Wenger makes a habit of picking up unknowns and making them into world-class players."

Former Arsenal boss **GEORGE GRAHAM** now knows his successor at Highbury doesn't always get it right!

"If Sven's been here to Molineux then I think he's been in disguise 'cos I've never seen him! I really enjoyed playing for the Under-21s and if they are short of left-sided players then I feel I have what it takes to do well for them. Sadly we do get somewhat over-looked here."

Maybe with Wolves' rise to the Premiership **LEE NAYLOR** might spot the England boss in the crowd.